The PENIS NAME Book

A GUIDE TO NAMING MAN'S BEST FRIEND

• DAVID ROSENTHAL AND SARYN CHORNEY •

 adamsmedia

Avon, Massachusetts

Published by
Adams Media, a division of F+W Media, Inc.
57 Littlefield Street, Avon, MA 02322. U.S.A.
www.adamsmedia.com

A Hollan Publishing, Inc. Concept

ISBN 10: 1-4405-0637-X
ISBN 13: 978-1-4405-0637-6
eISBN 10: 1-4405-0920-4
eISBN 13: 978-1-4405-0920-9

Printed in the United States of America.

10   9   8   7   6   5   4   3   2   1

Library of Congress Cataloging-in-Publication Data
Rosenthal, David.
The penis name book / David Rosenthal and Saryn Chorney.
p. cm.
ISBN 978-1-4405-0637-6
1. Penis—Humor. I. Chorney, Saryn. II. Title.
PN6231.P344R67 2010
818'.602—dc22
2010039128

This publication is designed to provide accurate and authoritative information with regard to the subject matter covered. It is sold with the understanding that the publisher is not engaged in rendering legal, accounting, or other professional advice. If legal advice or other expert assistance is required, the services of a competent professional person should be sought.
—From a *Declaration of Principles* jointly adopted by a Committee of the American Bar Association and a Committee of Publishers and Associations

Many of the designations used by manufacturers and sellers to distinguish their product are claimed as trademarks. Where those designations appear in this book and Adams Media was aware of a trademark claim, the designations have been printed with initial capital letters.

This book is available at quantity discounts for bulk purchases.
For information, please call 1-800-289-0963.

Dedication
To Goliath.

ACKNOWLEDGMENTS

We would like to thank Holly Schmidt and Allan Penn at Hollan Publishing for inspiring this book and making it happen. A big thank you to the people at Adams Media, particularly Brendan O'Neill and Katie Corcoran Lytle, whose advice, support, and tireless work made this book possible.

CONTENTS

Introduction
WHY NAME A PENIS?

As soon as a little boy discovers his wiener he realizes that there's power in his penis—and he quickly learns that displaying it will get him noticed. It might draw out a laugh, or elicit a scream, but reaction is bound to be strong. Just touching his penis (or somebody else's for that matter) will get yells of, "Don't play with that thing!" Clearly, the penis has a mysterious power and once a boy hits puberty, he starts to understand what that mystery is all about. A teenager's raging hormones and the rampant boners that they cause become all-consuming, causing blood and sensibility to rush from his head into his crotch. Even as he gets older and his boners become less frequent, his penis still remains his priority.

So why is a guy's penis the most important thing in his life? Where does the obsession come from? After all, it seems like everything a man does is for his penis's pleasure. For example, why do guys play sports? So they can impress girls who will hopefully play with their penises. Why do guys learn to play the guitar? In the hope that groupies will play with their penises. Why do guys get up in the morning, sit in traffic, and work at jobs they hate? So they can make money, which will hopefully impress someone enough that she'll play with their penises. If it was socially acceptable and paid the rent a lot of guys would probably masturbate as a career.

So, after all the special penis in your life has done for you, it's time to give it the name it deserves. But words like *dick*, *cock*, and *schlong* are just slang terms that could describe any random penis you meet on the street. Besides, you wouldn't want to call a friendly penis something so vulgar. After all, we give our friends nicknames, we name our pets, and some people even name their cars for God's sake. Whether the penis in question is your own or belongs to a friend of yours, the truth is that you are thinking about a penis that you care about. And when you care about something, you give it a name out of respect—and so you don't confuse it with any other penises that you know. To help you choose an appropriate name for that special dick in your life, we've provided a simple ratings system that rates each name's coolness and desirability. Each entry is accompanied by an icon of a penis in one of five states of arousal. The worst penises with the least recommended names will get a picture of a floppy and flaccid penis. Bigger boners continue up the scale until reaching the long and strong top-ranked hard-on. Our arousal-based system is highly scientific and should be considered the standard method in the penis-naming field.

People name penises for a variety of reasons. Perhaps that penis has never had a name and needs its first christening. In this case you should be honored. Perhaps the penis currently has a soft name and needs a new, hard moniker, or maybe its name just doesn't do it justice. In this case you have the special responsibility of righting a wronged dong. Whatever the reason, that penis needs a name, and the responsibility of naming it is yours. Congratulations! And good luck!

THE HISTORY OF PENIS NAMING

Before choosing a name, it's important to examine how penises have been considered and treated in an historical context. Here, we give you the play-by-play of the penis throughout time, and you'll come face-to-face with some historically notable penises.

PENIS AS POWER

Let's start by taking a look at how different people have viewed their society's members. Taking a look at how penises have been depicted historically may inspire your penis-naming abilities.

PAGANS

The oldest representation of a penis is a 28,000-year-old carved stone phallus found in a cave in Germany. Also found inside this same cave was the oldest known Venus figurine—a carved, buxom statuette of a nude woman. Are these the earliest evidence of a dildo and pornography, or were they fertility charms believed to have spiritual power? Scientists may never know the answer, but what they do know is that early humans recognized the contradiction that the penis presents. On the one hand, prehistoric man had only the most basic understanding of anatomy and biology, but they recognized the penis's connection to creation and the mystery of life and gave it a godlike reverence. On the other hand, they realized that a force of nature with a dark motive—aka lust—drives the penis. The same power that was the source for love and life could and did overwhelm men with unchecked aggression and uncontrollable behavior that led to violence and destruction. Unfortunately, some of today's men are indistinguishable from our less evolved ancestors.

HEBREWS

An important milestone in the history of the penis is the commandment of circumcision that God gave to the Hebrews. The ritual cutting of the penis's foreskin at eight days old represents a man's covenant with God, and is an act of devotion to his maker. Despite some modern-day controversy over circumcision's necessity and safety, it has become a common secular practice for most twentieth-century American males. Men may cringe at the thought of blood—especially in that "sacred" spot—but women who have had a monthly period for most of their lives may not be so sympathetic to men who were too young to even remember the experience of being cut.

GREEKS AND ROMANS

Ancient Greeks and Romans are lauded for establishing civilizations consisting of the highly developed art, poetry, drama, and philosophy that are the basis for today's Western culture, but they were also obsessed with sex and seem more comfortable with it than we are today. Erotic boudoir paintings, nude statues, and naked wrestling were pretty commonplace in the Mediterranean. In addition, both Greek and Roman mythology abounds with ribald stories of horny gods having sex with men and women, often forcefully, to satisfy their carnal desires. For gods and men, sex was seen as the source for power, and the penis was seen both as the source of sex and as the strongest representation of sexual power. Penises were frequently depicted in the art of the time, and phallic symbols were even used in religious ceremonies. Today, it's not common to witness a religious rite involving a penis, but quite a few guys have prayed to God that a night out will lead to sex.

CHRISTIANS

Many Christians suffer from a case of penis anxiety due to sex's confusing dichotomy. Is sex sinfully bad or just very, very good? Well, virginity is considered the purest form of holiness, as represented by Jesus Christ's mother, the Virgin Mary. It's inferred that sex inhibits one's intimacy with God—which is why priests and nuns take a vow of chastity—and the penis is the instrument of sex. When the penis takes a virgin's hymen, it robs her of her purity as well. Therefore the penis is a source of evil, something that cuts off a direct link to God. It's a small step forward to say that the penis is a tool of the devil.

Great, but here is where the confusion comes in. Christians are expected to avoid sin by waiting until marriage to have sex, at which point the husband and wife are instructed to have lots of kids. Sex, which was a sin, now becomes a revered act—and Christians are struck with a conundrum. How can they celebrate life, love, and marriage, which are considered virtues, while sex, which is a necessary element of being fruitful and growing a family, is frequently considered a sin? The poor penis is stuck in the middle of this problem. What would Jesus do? I think he'd want everyone to love their penis as they love themselves.

FAMOUS PENISES

From Adam and Eve to Bill and Monica, famous men and the women who love them have been getting in trouble for millennia due to penises run amok. Read on to hear about some of the most famous. . . .

RASPUTIN'S PENIS

Rasputin was a Russian mystic, thought by some to have supernatural abilities, who became a confidant of the last czar and czarina, Nicholas II and Alexandra of Russia. Unfortunately, his influence over the emperor and empress also earned him many enemies among Russia's noblemen, who assassinated him in grisly fashion in 1916. It's believed that the murderers castrated the mad monk, but the official autopsy report has been lost to antiquity, so the facts are unclear. The story goes that a maid discovered the penis and held on to it for a few years until sometime in the 1920s. The relic then somehow ended up in Paris, where it was worshipped as a fertility charm by a group of Russian expatriate women. One of Rasputin's daughters retrieved the family jewels and brought the penis with her to California, where it stayed until her death in 1977. It eventually landed in the lap of an auction house that, after close analysis, determined the "penis" was actually a dried-out sea cucumber. Gross!

NAPOLEON'S PENIS

After Napoleon died in exile on the island of Saint Helena, the doctor who performed the autopsy removed Napoleon's penis and gave it to a priest. In a bizarre twist, the priest was murdered, the victim of a blood vendetta, and the penis was passed from collector to collector; it was even put on public display in New York City in 1927. The penis was eventually sold at auction (the apparent destiny of famous penises), where it was bought by, of all people, a New Jersey urologist who happened to be a collector of macabre objects, such as Abraham Lincoln's bloodstained collar. To this day Napoleon's penis remains in the possession of the urologist's family. Attention all famous men: Do not fall asleep in your urologist's office or your manhood might end up part of his collection.

Now that you have a PhD in penis studies, you're closer than ever to finding a name for that penis. But first let's take a look at the types of slang words you should avoid when choosing a meaningful nickname for your prick.

HOW TO CHOOSE: FINDING THE RIGHT NAME FOR YOUR LITTLE FRIEND

You wouldn't name your kid "kiddo" or "honey," so why would you settle for a penis name like "dick"? Using playground slang words to refer to that special sausage is boring and lazy. Each penis deserves a memorable name that reflects the distinctive qualities that make it unique. So, before you get naming, hold on for just a second. There are slang terms you need to be aware of and naming rules that we strongly advise you to follow. Need specifics? Read on. . . .

PENIS SLANG

There are plenty of slang words for the male genitalia. The word *penis* comes from the Latin word meaning "tail." Maybe that's why guys are called "dogs." You shouldn't pull on a dog's tail and, likewise, tugging on a guy's "tail" might get you bit—but not necessarily in a bad way. There are many common names for the penis, all of which you should know before you start naming.

DICK

Richard was—and is—a very common name, which is often shortened to "Dick." Over time, *Dick* came to be a term that referred to the average person. *Dick* was also the name for a riding whip. No one knows for sure how the word became synonymous with the penis, but it makes sense to us because every average Dick had better learn to use his dick properly whether he wants to ride a filly or a stallion.

COCK

This slang term is a reference to a man's thrusting hips looking like a rooster's strut. One of the original meanings of the word *cock* denoted a type of spout or pipe that was used for channeling liquids, like a water tap. It's not hard to imagine that a creative kid in the schoolyard would put two and two together and devise a handy slang term.

PHALLUS

Phallus is now often used as a general term for *penis*, but the original Greek word actually referred to a type of image—either pictorial or sculptural—of the penis, which was carried during ancient festivals of Dionysus, symbolizing virility.

PUTZ AND SCHMUCK

Yiddish has a veritable treasure chest full of penis slang words. *Putz* and *schmuck* are vulgar words for *penis* that have been adopted into English to mean "idiot" or "jerk." Yiddish also gave English (and Beavis and Butthead of course) the word *schlong*, which translates to "snake."

SO HOW DO YOU CHOOSE?

Now that some background has been established, it's time to take a look at John "Penis" Doe and figure out what to call him. In order to choose the appropriate name for the penis at hand you need to consider a few things. After all, not just any pecker moniker will do. Just as every guy is unique, each penis is a special individual in how it looks, how it behaves, and in how you feel about it. The areas to consider are: physical characteristics, personality, and your relationship to the lil' sucker. So, always remember: **Physical + Personality + Relationship = The Perfect Penis Name.**

PHYSICAL

Let's be honest. Looks count and you need to take them into consideration when naming that special penis in your life. Considering the following:

- Are you naming a big donkey dick or a modest mouse?
- Is it dark meat or white?
- Is it long and lean or short and stubby?

A penis's physical characteristics include its shape, length, girth, and color, and even smell and taste should be taken into account. A penis's proportions—its "body shape" if you will—differs from dick to dick. Finally, some dicks are just more beautiful than others, and attractiveness shouldn't be disregarded. Be superficial and consider all of these physical traits when choosing a name.

PERSONALITY

The second important factor to consider is the personality of the guy, which correlates with the personality of the penis. Does the penis Hulk-out in arousal with the merest glance? Is it an endurance specialist able to run an all-night marathon? Maybe it's an innocent dick new to the love game that is eager to learn from a sexy sensei. This is the time to be a penis shrink, so turn on your powers of analysis and figure out what makes this dick tick.

PHYSICAL MEETS PERSONALITY

This is the appropriate place for a discussion about how physical and personality traits affect and interact with each other. But before we get there, keep in mind that a large penis isn't automatically good, and a small penis isn't automatically bad. That said, in case you're interested in what the ladies are looking for, according to a nonscientific Internet survey, most women report that the ideal penis size is between 7¼ and 8¼ inches long and 6¼ to 6½ inches in circumference. It's generally believed that bigger is better, but ultimately size preference is different for everyone.

Okay, back to business. We're sure you've realized that guys who discover they have a big dick at a young age will often grow an equally large ego. And as soon as girls discover this guy's big size and stroke his uh, *ego*, he will turn into a truly big dick. He will use his crotch as a crutch instead of developing a true personality. Often the best big dicks are ones that developed late in puberty, so the guy has spent some time developing other things like charisma, a sense of humor, and an education. His well roundedness plus his plus-size penis makes him one hell of a catch, and his dick deserves a great name. Keep these factors in mind when naming a big penis.

A guy with a small dick will hopefully learn to fill out his other traits and, with any luck, his cock may even get bigger as he ages. This guy will ideally work hard on his bedroom technique in order to compensate for his lack of girth. He'll probably try really hard to impress the ladies and will work hard to prove his worth. Because if a woman isn't getting any satisfaction from a tiny penis, even if it's owned by the sweetest guy in the world, both the penis and its partner are going to be left frustrated and unfulfilled. Ladies: Remember that a particular key might seem good, but it's worthless if it doesn't fit in the lock. You need to find a penis that is the right fit for you.

RELATIONSHIPS: FROM HERE TO ETERNITY OR GONE WITH THE WIND?

Once you take physicality and personality into account, it's time to determine what your relationship is like. Take into consideration how the penis acts around you. Think about your relationship with the penis. Is it a friend or foe? Are you planning on spending a lot of time with it? If it's a penis you want in your life, you'll want to find a name that is flattering to and fitting for the guy who owns it. Remember, if the owner of the penis isn't a fan of the name you choose, he might have trouble getting it up—which puts everyone in a bad spot. Also, avoid names that you may find funny now, but you'll get sick of after a month. Mortimer used to be a cool name for babies, but not so much nowadays. So find a name for the penis that will stand the test of time, or at least the length of your relationship.

Of course, if you're choosing a name for a penis you don't plan on seeing again, or even one that you don't like, feel free to name it whatever you want! Maybe it was a penis you met on a one-night-stand, but it was so memorable that it deserves to be commemorated. Maybe it was an awful penis and needs a name that fits when you recite the horror story as a warning to your friends. In this case, you don't have to worry about seeing these particular penises again, so you can go ahead and call them whatever name you want to in the story you tell the next day.

Okay, you've been patient, but enough with all this foreplay; you're ready for some real action. The names in this book are separated into familiar categories that should satisfy you whether you're a movie buff or a gear head who needs a name for your latest hot *rod*. Just take your time, start slow, and see which name grows on you.

Cinematic Names

The penis rating system

1 2 3 4 5

If you're looking to name a penis worthy of the silver screen, this is the chapter for you. Sit your shooting star down on the casting couch and choose a name inspired by actors, famous characters, and movies. Find a cock-buster that will give you a big opening weekend.

APOLLO CREED

ORIGIN: The world champion boxer Apollo Creed was Sly Stallone's titular character's foil in *Rocky I* and *Rocky II*, but eventually they made up and became best friends. Hey, nobody claimed the *Rocky* movies made any sense. Apollo Creed was made famous by actor Carl Weathers as much for his bombastic portrayal of the patriotic boxer as for his cut-from-stone and oiled-all-over body. Apollo's extreme self-confidence was also his downfall when he barely defeated Rocky in the first movie.

REASON: An Apollo Creed is a top performing American-made penis. Apollo's skills include making dramatic entrances and looking fantastic poking out of red, white, and blue boxer shorts.

RATING:

BEETLEJUICE

ORIGIN: There was a time when director Tim Burton directed truly original movies, not just adaptations. In 1988, he created *Beetlejuice*, a wonderfully weird life-after-death story that featured a hunky young Alec Baldwin and sexy Geena Davis as a recently departed couple, and Michael Keaton as a troublemaking "ghost with the most."

REASON: *Beetlejuice* is the name of the hair-trigger wiener that only needs to hear his name said three times in order to come. Worse, a *Beetlejuice* is nearly impossible to get rid of once he's been shown a good time, so his partner probably needs an exorcism—or a restraining order—to make him disappear.

RATING:

BEN-HUR

ORIGIN: *Ben-Hur* (1959) is the Oscar-winning story of a man who overcame incredible odds to become the champion charioteer of the Roman Colosseum. The movie starred Charlton Heston and inspired every Hollywood sword and sandal epic ever since, especially *Gladiator* (2000)—another Best Picture winner.

REASON: One of the biggest fighters of all time, a Ben-Hur is a valiant opponent in the bedroom. This hero treats a woman like his chariot and rides her around the room. Giddy-up!

RATING:

THE BIG LEBOWSKI

ORIGIN: Starring Jeff Bridges as a slacker antihero for our bizarre modern times, the *Big Lebowski* (1998) is a surreal trip through Los Angeles. Lebowski would prefer to just bowl in his favorite robe with his buddies and avoid looking for a job, but he's drawn into a weird adventure in his search for a stolen rug (it really pulls the room together).

REASON: The best part about being or being with a Lebowski is that he's low maintenance—though, he does prefer his bowling balls waxed. A man with a Lebowski likes sex coupled with a joint and a white Russian. So, just chill out, toke up, and relax with this mellow Dude. And remember, this dick abides.

RATING:

BLUTO

ORIGIN: *Animal House* is an iconic 1978 film that has influenced many subsequent comedies as well as every freshman with a "College" sweatshirt. This is the movie that made John Belushi a mega-star for his character Bluto.

REASON: Inspired by John Belushi's famous food-spitting scene, this is a good name for a fat cock that makes a mess—maybe in a lady's face. Unfortunately, lots of frat boys are inspired by Bluto and follow in his toga- and sandal-clad footsteps. The futon of a guy with a Bluto will probably be notched with several Roman numerals.

RATING:

BRUCE LEE

ORIGIN: Bruce Lee's first introduction to Americans was on the TV series *The Green Hornet* as the martial arts master, Kato. He gained international star status postmortem when the film *Enter the Dragon* (1973) was released after his tragic death. He introduced the martial arts to the forefront of popular culture more than any other man.

REASON: This dick earns its name by coming hard and fast with powerful thrusts. To be worthy of Bruce's spirit and athletic prowess, you or your partner must be able to get it on in all kinds of crazy positions and perform wild moves most people have never even seen before.

RATING:

CHEWBACCA

ORIGIN: Han Solo's tall and hairy copilot is one of *Star Wars'* most popular heroes, despite the fact that he's a seven-foot-tall alien covered in shaggy fur who only speaks through a series of grunts and howls.

REASON: Chewbacca is loyal and brave, kind of like a dog. Some people are so into him that they like to dress up like a Wookie and hump, but that's another story. You could call a really furry dick a Chewbacca.

(And you can call a furry's dick
Chewbacca.)

RATING:

CONAN

ORIGIN: Conan the Barbarian first
appeared in comic books in 1932
but gained international fame when
Arnold Schwarzenegger portrayed
him in his 1982 breakthrough role.

REASON: The owner of a Conan
is a strapping warrior who uses his
"sword" to impress girls. Only a
horny member big enough to be held
with two hands deserves this name.
He may not be that smart, but his
Eastern European-esque accent is
kind of cute. Lowered defenses—
and Red Sonja panties—allow this
dick to conquer!

RATING:

DANNY DEVITO

ORIGIN: Danny DeVito has been a
Hollywood favorite for decades. He
has played comedic scoundrels in
movies (*Romancing the Stone*, 1984)
and on TV (*It's Always Sunny in Philadelphia*), but his most beloved role
is probably as Arnold Schwarzenegger's brother in *Twins*.

REASON: A Danny DeVito can be
easily mistaken for a Bilbo Baggins
(see Literary Names). Both come
in small packages, but it's the size
of the package in their shorts that
matters. Just like the unsavory
characters Danny DeVito has played
throughout his career, a Danny
DeVito penis is a big dick. So don't
discriminate based on height. For
one thing, a Danny DeVito can fit
snugly between a lady's legs, and
secondly he's taller lying on his back
than standing up.

RATING:

DARTH VADER

ORIGIN: Darth Vader terrorized Han and Luke in the *Star Wars* trilogy and quickly became one of the greatest onscreen villains of all time. His frightening reputation became tragically epic when we learned there was an actual man behind the black mask.

REASON: A man with a Darth Vader earned this nickname because he wants to in-"vade" those "darth" places . . . you know, the planet "Ur-anus"? Still not getting it? The most evil Jedi around wants to put his *lightsaber* in some unlucky girl's *dark side!* Nothing wrong with that if you're both into it, but make sure to put a helmet on that thing before he launches an attack.

RATING: RANGES FROM 🐚 TO 🍆 DEPENDING ON YOUR SEXUAL PROCLIVITIES.

DIRK DIGGLER

ORIGIN: In *Boogie Nights* (1997), one of Mark Wahlberg's rare great performances, he plays Dirk Diggler, the naive but fantastically endowed young man who rises up (pun intended) through the porn industry of the late 1970s. The movie is based on the life of infamous adult film star John Holmes.

REASON: A Dirk Diggler is no stunt cock; this is the real thingy. Former bad boy Marky Mark himself brought this stunningly large penis to life, and only porn-star-status-worthy wieners deserve this name. Feel, feel, feel, feel his good vibrations while you do the horizontal boogie.

RATING: 🍆

DIRTY HARRY

ORIGIN: After Clint Eastwood played a Western gunslinger, but before he started riding around in a truck with an orangutan, he was Dirty Harry, a San Francisco cop on the hunt for a serial killer named Scorpio.

REASON: Known to shoot first and ask questions later, this dirty dude breaks the rules—and makes a mess. A guy with a Dirty Harry was the smelly kid in school, but instead of growing up and getting clean, the smell has only grown stronger. Stay away from him!

RATING:

DOCTOR DETROIT

ORIGIN: The comedy *Doctor Detroit* (1983) stars Dan Aykroyd as a man with a dual identity. He is a timid professor who gets wrapped up in the world of high-class prostitution and becomes an over-the-top pimp with a fake metal hand and awful accent.

REASON: The wiener worthy of this name appears timid on the surface, but when the pants come off, he's a real pimp-daddy in the sack. His owner's iron grip on his lover's ass will make it easy for any woman to stand by her man, so keep your socializing to a minimum and just get down to playing doctor. (Especially for penises in the state of Michigan.)

RATING:

DONNIE DARKO

ORIGIN: *Donnie Darko* (2001) is a disturbingly good sci-fi film that stars Jake Gyllenhaal as the titular character, a suburban teen with alarming visions of the end of the world. A man in a scary rabbit costume gives apocalyptic messages to Donnie. Yikes!

REASON: This is an appropriate name for a dark *fore*-skinned fellow, or possibly for a cute but odd penis next door (who may or may not be able to time-travel). If he—or you—are one of the former, enjoy your night. Ladies, if he's the latter, keep your costume in the closet when making out. He's not into furries.

RATING: 🍆

THE ELEPHANT MAN

ORIGIN: *The Elephant Man* (1980) is a drama adapted from the true story of a real man who lived with a severe body deformity. He was found in a London freak show, abused and dehumanized. Everyone assumed he was dumb, but through the kindness of new friends he reveals a deep spirituality and intelligence.

REASON: Huge? Yes. Terrifying to look at? Yes. The Elephant Man is one ugly sucker. This one is for lovers of scary movies and freak fetishists only.

RATING: 🍆🍆

FLOUNDER

ORIGIN: Flounder, the overweight and neurotic freshman in *Animal House* (1978), is the subject of abuse from most of his school's upperclassmen, including his own fraternity brothers.

REASON: This name is reserved for the penis of the lamest of chunky college freshman. When a girl encounters a floppy, flaccid dick that has no clue what to do with itself, she's hooked herself a Flounder. Throw him back: there are always more fish in the sea.

RATING: 🍆

FORREST GUMP

ORIGIN: *Forrest Gump* (1994) stars Tom Hanks as a slow but extra-special man who finds himself wrapped up in some of the most significant political and cultural events of the late twentieth century.

REASON: Like his movie character namesake, the owner of a Forrest Gump has the annoying tendency of popping in and out of his lady's life at the oddest moments. A woman can't escape him no matter how hard she tries, because he's so fast on his feet. Plus, that box of chocolates he keeps offering isn't cute anymore; it's just annoying and makes a girl fat.

RATING:

THE GIMP

ORIGIN: The Gimp from *Pulp Fiction* (1994) was kept in a box by the sexually deviant cop and pawnshop owner who kidnapped and terrorized anyone who was unlucky enough to find themselves in their grasp.

REASON: A man with a dick named the Gimp won't talk much due to the leather mask he wears, but silence can be golden when all a woman wants is a crazy night of ass-slapping fun. Slapping *his* ass, that is. Yes, the Gimp is a glutton for punishment so, ladies, feel free to play out your wildest dominatrix fantasies. Grab your favorite riding crop, put on that rubber suit hidden in the back of the closet, and bring out the Gimp!

RATING:

THE GLADIATOR

ORIGIN: *Gladiator* (2000) is the Oscar-winning story of Maximus (played by Russell Crowe), a general who became a slave, and a slave who became a gladiator, and a gladiator who defied an emperor. That's according to the movie poster, but the movie is really just an excuse for fight scenes with sweaty, shirtless guys.

REASON: Aka *Penis Maximus*; the champion of the cock-a-seum, the

Gladiator is a strong, loyal, and huge sword. This warrior's performance gets a thumbs-up from the empress.

RATING:

THE GODFATHER

ORIGIN: *The Godfather* is widely considered one of the greatest films of all time. It's an epic tale of one mafia family's dominance over the New York world of crime throughout the twentieth century, when the Sopranos were still just a twinkle in Don Corleone's eye.

REASON: A night with the Godfather is an offer no one wants to refuse. The boss of the bedroom, any woman will gladly kneel down and kiss his cock ring. However, if you've watched any movies about the mob, you know that relationships with the Godfather usually end poorly. Enjoy it while it lasts.

RATING:

THE GREAT DICTATOR

ORIGIN: *The Great Dictator* (1940) was a satire of Nazism and Hitler written, directed, and starring Charlie Chaplin. The movie was released years before the United States entered World War II, but it is credited as being an influence on the country's condemnation of Nazi Germany and a catalyst for America's decision to fight.

REASON: This is the perfect name for a dick that is attached to a guy who is uber-demanding in the bedroom. He is intense, high-strung, and prone to fits of megalomania, but his charisma is irresistible. His partner gladly obeys his instructions, because playing follow the leader gets her off just as much as it excites him. He's a dick, but that's the point. Right?

RATING:

HAN SOLO

ORIGIN: Harrison Ford became a household name after portraying Han Solo, *Star Wars'* most famous space cowboy.

REASON: *Star Wars* may be a geeky guy's wet dream, but there is one huge reason for ladies to nerd out too, and that reason is the galaxy's ultimate bad boy, Han Solo. Han is the cinematic stand-in for that guy a mom warns her daughter not to date. Ladies know a man with a Han Solo is bad news, but they still can't resist letting him have his way with them in the back of a beat-up *Millennium Falcon*. A man with this dick won't send flowers the next day and will forget most girls' names, but years later, when that lucky lady is safely settled down and slipping into bed with Mr. Right, she'll think of her tryst with the man with a Han Solo to launch her orgasm into orbit.

RATING:

HAPPY GILMORE

ORIGIN: Adam Sandler played the titular hero of *Happy Gilmore* (1996), the most successful hockey-player-turned-golfer comedy of all time.

REASON: This penis is the perfect caddy for a guy who avoids *fore*-play and gets right to the big strokes. He's immature, but he makes up for his lack of smoothness with lots of enthusiasm for a hole-in-one. He loves his grandma, which is sweet, but that's not a strong enough reason on its own for a lady to make him her Big Daddy.

RATING:

INDIANA JONES

ORIGIN: *Raiders of the Lost Ark* is the movie that introduced the whip-cracking archaeologist Indiana Jones to the world. Released in 1981, in addition to making history cool, *Raiders* introduced a new generation to the type of adventure stories that director Steven Spielberg and producer George Lucas read in comic books and saw onscreen in the 1950s.

REASON: It should come as no surprise that a large number of girls who came of age during the '80s have a fetish for whips, leather (jackets), and fedoras due to Harrison Ford's Indiana Jones character. He single-handedly got more archaeologists laid than previously thought possible. This name is appropriate for a dick that is long enough to crack like a whip, or for the member of anyone who is especially adventurous in bed.

RATING:

ITALIAN STALLION

ORIGIN: Just like Sylvester Stallone's character, the Italian Stallion, *Rocky* was an underdog when it was released in theaters. But Rocky became the biggest hero in Philadelphia when the movie won the 1978 best picture Oscar and became the biggest box-office hit of the year. *Rocky* gave Stallone his "Stallion" nickname and his reputation from being a generously endowed stud. It turns out the film wasn't exaggerating, as audiences saw when a Stallone porno film was released after *Rocky's* success. What was it called? *The Italian Stallion* of course.

REASON: Yo, this powerful goomba usually hails from Philly, Staten

Island, or down at the Jersey Shore. He'll come back in the ring one, two, three—hell, six times, until he's taken some lucky lady over the top.

RATING: 1

JACK SPARROW

ORIGIN: Captain Jack Sparrow (played by Johnny Depp) is the roguish pirate hero of the *Pirates of the Caribbean* series. He is a silver-tongued trickster who prefers to talk his way out of a dangerous situation rather than fight. Depp famously modeled the usually rum-drunk Sparrow character after Rolling Stones guitarist Keith Richards, based on his feeling that pirates were the rock stars of their time.

REASON: After a night of drinking salty dogs and rum punches a woman might be convinced that a man sporting a Jack Sparrow is a rock star based on his karaoke ver-

sion of "Satisfaction." Oh well, she can pretend for a night, can't she? Ladies, go ahead and play Elizabeth Swann to this guy's Jack Sparrow, and let him give you a Jolly Rogering.

RATING:

JAMES BOND (OR 007)

ORIGIN: British secret agent James Bond—a dapper Englishman who mixes deadly efficiency with sexy style—first appeared in a series of novels by Ian Fleming but became internationally well known through his portrayal in film. Beginning with *Dr. No* in 1962, the Bond film franchise became wildly popular and made Sean Connery, the first actor to take on the 007 role, a household name.

REASON: "Bond . . . James Bond." Any guy who can pull off that line without sounding cheesy may have a penis worthy of the title 007. A man with a James Bond is an Englishman who is as smooth as a shaken martini. He could also be an irresistibly sexy one-night stand who wants to put his Goldfinger in your Octopussy.

RATING:

JAWS

ORIGIN: *Jaws* is cinema's famous great white shark that has terrified movie audiences for decades. The first movie scared beachgoers out of the water in 1975 and was such a huge hit that it initiated the modern era of summer blockbusters.

REASON: Jaws is a big dick that hunts the endless sea of bars and lounges searching for his prey. This shark knows there are plenty of fish out there so he never settles for just one, but if a woman lets him swim around in her aquarium, she should prepare for a surprise attack that will leave her wet and maybe a little scared—in a good way.

RATING:

KEYSER SÖZE

ORIGIN: Keyser Söze is the much discussed, but rarely seen, villain from *The Usual Suspects* (1995) who was apparently pulling the strings of a wide-ranging crime syndicate. Audiences were left shocked by the revelatory twist ending.

REASON: Keyser Söze is a mysterious member. Evidence for this legendary big dick is written on bathroom stall walls and whispered about in ladies locker rooms, but no one seems to ever have any firsthand experience with it. If you find one—or if you have one—be sure to put it to good use.

RATING:

LANDO CALRISSIAN

ORIGIN: Billy Dee Williams was both the coolest and only black guy in space according to the *Star Wars* universe. His character Lando Calrissian betrayed his frenemy Han Solo in *The Empire Strikes Back* (1980) but later redeemed himself in *Return of the Jedi* (1983).

REASON: You have to be as smooth as Billy Dee Williams to pull off wearing a blue cape and leather boots. Lando's famous pick-up lines include "You look absolutely beautiful. You truly belong here with us among the clouds." A man with a Lando Calrissian is such a charmer that all the ladies want to wear their sexy slave-Leia costumes for him.

RATING:

LETHAL WEAPON

ORIGIN: The action series *Lethal Weapon* stars Mel Gibson and Danny Glover as opposites-attract police detectives who partner up to take down a never-ending series of bad guys in Los Angeles.

REASON: This piece is no pea-shooter; it's more like a bazooka in the bedroom. A woman will need to get a gun license to handle the Lethal Weapon, so put on that sexy bad-cop uniform and hang onto the key to those handcuffs.

RATING:

LONG DUK DONG (AKA "THE DONGER")

ORIGIN: The Donger was, by far, the smoothest character in the John Hughes classic *Sixteen Candles* (1984), not only introducing himself to Molly Ringwald with a classic pick-up line ("What's happening hot stuff?"), but also getting the most action in the movie (with a big-boobed jock chick named Marlene).

REASON: Politically correct people might frown at calling a guy's dick "the Donger," but you'll be very happy you let this "exchange student" help you with your sex-ed homework. You might even end up married. "Mwarried? Yes, mwarried."

RATING: 🍆

THE LORD OF THE COCK RINGS

ORIGIN: *The Lord of the Rings* trilogy of movies was one of the greatest undertakings in Hollywood history. The epic films took three years to make and had a cast of thousands on hand to create the massive world of Middle Earth. The result of all this hard work was seventeen Oscars, billions of dollars, and making pointy ears and hairy feet sexy.

REASON: The Lord of the Cock Rings belongs to a guy who decorates his Johnson with jewelry, and I don't mean the bedazzled variety. Why use a cock ring? Well, this little strip of metal or plastic is placed at the base of the penis to restrict blood flow, which keeps a man harder longer and makes a woman beg for more. A good Lord puts that big boner to use on his fair maiden.

RATING: 🍆

LUKE SKYWALKER

ORIGIN: Luke is a simple farm boy who becomes a space-samurai in the epic *Star Wars* series.

REASON: A man with a Luke Skywalker is the polar opposite of one with a Han Solo. A man with a Luke is innocent, trustworthy, and forthright—all of which makes him totally lame. He barely knows how to handle his lightsaber (zing!), he's always whining, *and* he kissed his sister! Gross! The sexual force is not strong with this one.

RATING:

MARSELLUS WALLACE

ORIGIN: Marsellus is the crime boss of *Pulp Fiction* (1994) who is on the hunt for Bruce Willis's character Butch, until Butch saves them both from a pair of rednecked rapists.

REASON: A man with a Marsellus Wallace does not look like a bitch, so a girl shouldn't try to fuck him like one. He's a badass gangster who lives by an honorable code, but if you mess with him he'll get medieval on your ass.

RATING:

MAVERICK

ORIGIN: *Top Gun* (1986) stars Tom Cruise as the hot and independent Navy airman, Maverick. The movie is now a relic of the Cold War, but Cruise has remained in the hearts of teenage girls for fighting off Soviet jet fighters while seducing Kelly McGillis and frolicking on the beach with Val Kilmer.

REASON: A girl will never lose that loving feeling after strapping herself around the engines of this high-flying stud. This cock-sure pilot is easily identified because he's always wearing aviator sunglasses and is accompanied by his wing-balls, Goose and Iceman.

RATING:

MCLOVIN

ORIGIN: McLovin is the underdog hero from *Superbad* (2007) whose choice of name for his fake ID leads him into an adventure with two cops and one horny redheaded chick.

REASON: A man with a McLovin is a nerdy, but lovable, virgin. The dude who is used to getting lots of ass never appreciates what he has. Someone with a McLovin, on the other hand, will be eternally grateful when a girl allows him into her pants, and he'll always remember his first. Of course a McLovin will be done pretty quickly because he has a lifetime of anticipation that has built up, but he'll be ready to go again in about ten minutes. And then ten minutes later . . . and ten minutes after that. . . .

RATING:

MINI ME

ORIGIN: First appearing in *Austin Powers: The Spy Who Shagged Me* (1999), Dr. Evil's tiny doppelganger either pushed little people's interests

forward or sent them hurtling backwards, depending on your view of Mike Myers's comedy.

REASON: A Mini Me is probably incredibly small, so this is an insulting nickname for a penis. Yeah, yeah, yeah, women tell guys that "it's not the size of the boat, it's the motion in the ocean," and "a sense of humor is more important," but everyone knows that small dicks suck regardless of what a man does with it or how funny and sweet he is. Bottom line, don't put up with a tiny schween unless the guy attached to it is rich and his randy, well-hung Brazilian pool boy is discreet.

RATING:

MR. PINK

ORIGIN: *Reservoir Dogs* blew the doors off the film industry of the mid-1990s with a hail of bullets. Quentin Tarantino's first film inspired dozens of imitators trying to replicate its distinctive combination of pop-culture references, charismatic criminals, and extreme violence.

REASON: We feel sorry for anyone who encounters a Mr. Pink. Inspired by the annoying character played by Steve Buscemi, a man with a Mr. Pink is a whiny, complaining douchebag. The first clear sign that he's a loser is when he refuses to tip the waitress at the restaurant, the second when he sticks you with the bill. Few people know what a Mr. Pink looks like because no girl is willing to admit she slept with such a loser.

RATING: 🌀

MUFASA

ORIGIN: *The Lion King* (1994) is a beloved modern classic of animation produced by Disney. Mufasa—who was voiced by the velvet-toned James Earl Jones—is the father of the film's hero, Simba.

REASON: A Mufasa is the undisputed ruler of the bedroom; this Lion King doesn't have any problem making a kitty purr. This is a good, if obvious, title for the penis of a feline-fetishist. He just needs to remember to wear his royal "robe" to avoid completing the circle of life and creating a litter of kitties. Long live the king!

RATING: 🍆

NORMAN BATES

ORIGIN: *Psycho* is a terrifying psychological horror film from the brilliant mind of Alfred Hitchcock. In the original 1960 film, Anthony Perkins plays the normal-seeming Norman Bates, a hotel owner who spends his nights dressing up like his dead mother and murdering pretty girls while they shower.

REASON: Danger! A Norman Bates belongs to a good-looking guy who seems nice, but he is actually a real creeper. He probably wears women's underwear and secretly spies on the girls he dates. Hopefully you'll see the warning signs before you get close enough to find out. Do *not* shower with this guy.

RATING: 🐚

PRIVATE BENJAMIN

ORIGIN: *Private Benjamin* is a classic comedy from 1980 starring Goldie Hawn as a spoiled woman who joins the army after the death of her husband on their wedding night. Despite her obvious mismatch with the service, *Private Benjamin* finds her inner soldier and her independence.

REASON: Private Benjamin is a penis that's up at attention every morning, ready to do a hundred pushups. While this soldier's gusto is easy to appreciate, his enthusiasm over the long-term can feel like an unwilling tour of duty. He should be properly disciplined by a partner who can teach him that a lady soldier deserves some R and R before she becomes Benjamin's POW.

RATING: 🦴

RAGING BULL

ORIGIN: *Raging Bull* (1980) is possibly the finest collaboration between director Martin Scorsese and star Robert De Niro. The film portrays the life of Jake La Motta, a boxer whose anger and insecurities derailed his road to success.

REASON: A champion in his young age, a Raging Bull's best days are now behind him. He's grown old, chubby, and slow, which makes him easy to spot at the bar. Women will want to avoid this angry and bitter former fighter and find a young heavy hitter instead.

RATING:

RAMBO

ORIGIN: *Rocky* (1976) put Sylvester Stallone on the map, but *Rambo* (aka *First Blood*, 1982) made him an international action hero. While the first *Rambo* film considered the plight of a shell-shocked Vietnam vet, the sequels were little more than mass blood orgies of a roided-up Stallone killing every thing in sight.

REASON: Like a one-man army, Rambo takes care of business in the bedroom. This is the right name for a penis that can take on multiple partners in one night. He's also not at all concerned if any of his partners are having their period. This may also be an appropriate name for a dick that scores a virgin's "First Blood."

RATING:

ROCKY HORROR

ORIGIN: *The Rocky Horror Picture Show* is a musical comedy that has become the most successful cult film in history. Released in 1975, the film still plays in theaters in special showings, to the joy of its fans— who dress up as characters from the film and interact with the movie's dialogue and dance scenes.

REASON: This is the most appropriate nickname for a sweet transvestite-pansexual-scientist penis. Though they are a rare find, if you hang around certain street corners in New York City and Hollywood, California, there's a chance you'll spend the weirdest night of your life with one of these very special Frank-N-Furters.

RATING:

SHAFT

ORIGIN: *Shaft* (1971) is an action thriller starring Richard Roundtree as John Shaft, a black detective who kills his way through a gaggle of racist whiteys in 1970s New York City.

REASON: The dude sporting a Shaft is a complicated man, but no one understands him better than his woman. *Shaft!* Big, black, and a badass mofo. *Shaft!* He's the coolest cat on the block. Can you dig it? *Shaft!* If so, then claim your *Shaft!* and go get laid.

RATING:

SHREK

ORIGIN: Voiced by comedian Mike Myers, Shrek is a gruff ogre with a heart of gold and a donkey for a best friend. *Shrek* (2001) has spawned three sequels and millions of awful attempts at a vaguely Scottish accent.

REASON: A Shrek sure is ugly, but boy is he a monster in the sack. This name is especially appropriate for an ogre who pillow-talks with a Scottish accent and is always trying to do you donkey-style. He may treat his partner like a princess, but if he's green, take him (and yourself) to a doctor immediately.

RATING:

SLIMER

ORIGIN: Slimer is the most popular ghost from the movie *Ghostbusters* (1984), mainly because he isn't really an evil spirit, just a gluttonous troublemaker. He went on to be one of the good guys in the Saturday-morning cartoon version of the movie.

REASON: In the dating world a Slimer belongs to a good guy who makes a big mess on his lover when he comes. No big deal, ladies! Just take the fact that he has so much love-juice to give as a compliment and keep extra moist-wipes next to the bed. Important note: If a woman who happens to be a squirter is dating a Slimer, she needs to make sure she doesn't cross the streams!

RATING:

STIFLER

ORIGIN: Seann William Scott's Stifler is the definitive high-school jock asshole from the *American Pie* comedy series.

REASON: A man with a Stifler is full of himself, a complete jerk, and has a nasty habit of accidentally swallowing misplaced come-in-a-cup. He is a tool, so be aware that this dick is probably using any girl just for sex. Every girl falls for a jerk sometime in her life, so ladies, feel free to go ahead and use this tool in return—if you're willing to put up with his high jinks.

RATING:

THE TERMINATOR

ORIGIN: *The Terminator* (1984) is a dystopian sci-fi film about a terrifying future full of killer robots that look like Arnold Schwarzenegger. The titular villain was a cyborg sent from the future to kill the mother of the human leader in an upcoming war against the robots. Watch out: Your computer may be trying to kill you.

REASON: A guy with a Terminator is an intense, foreign man of few words but lots of muscle—especially a big love muscle. Women don't sleep with him for the conversation; he's taken to bed because he has the power and endurance of a cyborg from the future sent back in time with the mission to pleasure. So what if he always finishes sex with his favorite catchphrase, spoken in an Austrian accent, "I'll come on your back." After all, the fate of the world depends on him hooking up.

RATING:

WILLY WONKA

ORIGIN: Gene Wilder (and later Johnny Depp) portrayed the whimsical man-child Willy Wonka, the kooky candy maker in the film adaptations of Roald Dahl's classic book *Charlie and the Chocolate Factory*. Willy Wonka ingeniously hid five golden tickets in his candy bars and the children who found them were invited to see his mysterious chocolate factory.

REASON: If you're lucky enough to have or find a willy that tastes like candy, congratulations: You've found the golden ticket—a Willy Wonka! Women will want to keep sucking on this tasty lollipop as if it's an everlasting gobstopper—though they probably won't want to play into his preference for top hats or orange-tinted little friends.

RATING:

THE WIZ

ORIGIN: The Wiz is the man behind the curtain in the 1978 film of the same name—an adaptation of the original Broadway musical and well-known movie *The Wizard of Oz*. He acts like a mighty sorcerer, but he's really a scared little man pretending to be much more than he is.

REASON: Women will realize they've been gazing through emerald-tinted beer goggles when they first see the Wiz stuffed down a not-so-lucky guy's pants. When they finally pull back the curtains—er, the sheets—all they find is a munchkin. Ladies, if you come across the Wiz, skip back on down the yellow brick road and try to find that hard Tin Man you were flirting with earlier in the night.

RATING:

Television Names

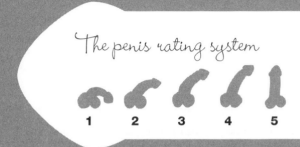

The penis rating system

1 2 3 4 5

Our favorite TV shows and characters are special to us because we let them into the privacy of our homes every week. This is why television is a good place to look for a name for the penis that we welcome into our bed on a regular basis. Plus, even a dick of below average size will appear larger if it's on your TV screen.

ALF

ORIGIN: ALF, the most famous Alien Life Form of the eighties, was traveling through space when he crash-landed in the Tanner family's garage and their lives, making the show one of TV's most memorable sitcoms. A short, wisecracking fur ball, ALF's favorite food is cat—a delicacy on his home planet Melmac—and he would frequently chase the family cat Lucky around the house.

REASON: ALF loves to eat "pussy," so ladies will always love ALF, even if he is short and covered in fur.

RATING:

BALKI BARTOKOMOUS

ORIGIN: Bronson Pinchot's character Balki from sitcom *Perfect Strangers* is an innocent and fun-loving immigrant who left his life as a shepherd on the island of Mypos to live with his neurotic cousin Larry Appleton in Chicago. Let the eighties-style high jinks begin!

REASON: There are two types of Balkis, and you may not know which one you have until you get up close and personal. If you're lucky, you've found yourself a Mediterranean Lothario to do the dance of joy with all night. On the other hand, you may be stuck with a dick that would rather be sleeping with his sheep.

RATING:

BARNEY

ORIGIN: Neil Patrick Harris began his career in the eighties as the sweet prodigy Dr. Doogie Howser, but his persona grew up and took a devilish turn in the self-referential role of NPH in the *Harold & Kumar* movies and especially as Barney, the dapper suit-wearing ladies' man of *How I Met Your Mother*. Barney is a highly intelligent and crafty womanizer who uses his Machiavellian skills to manipulate women out of their clothes and into his bed.

REASON: Barney is a penis found inside an expensive pair of pants. One way or another a Barney will have a lucky lady in her birthday suit before she knows it.

RATING:

BEAVER CLEAVER

ORIGIN: *Leave It to Beaver* is a classic American family sitcom, starring Jerry Mathers as Beaver Cleaver, one of TV's most lovable scamps. Beaver's naiveté would usually get him into trouble, but he was so cute nobody could stay mad at him.

REASON: A man with a Beaver Cleaver is so adorable, especially when he looks at a woman with those puppy dog eyes, but don't let

his boyish ways trick you. This dude is really a wild dog on the hunt for "beave." Go ahead and let him bury his bone.

RATING:

"BONER" STABONE

ORIGIN: The eighties sitcom *Growing Pains* is fondly remembered by most Gen-Xers for its mix of relatable family foibles and the antics of the show's three children. It may never be fully understandable how the censors allowed a character on an ABC prime-time show to be called "Boner," but thank the lord they did because a generation of teenage girls' personal growing pains were eased by late-night fantasies of being double-teamed by Kirk Cameron's character Mike Seaver and his best friend, Boner.

REASON: A girl's first Boner will be remembered fondly forever. A

Boner Stabone will never be the main character in the sitcom that is your sexual life. He's a penis that has a recurring guest star role in your bed every few weeks. He's your penis-friend with benefits. We don't recommend you play around with your boyfriend's best friend's Boner unless you're looking for more drama in your life.

RATING: 🍆

CAPTAIN KIRK

ORIGIN: The original *Star Trek* series was on air for only three seasons but went on to create one of the biggest science fiction franchises ever, with five additional spinoff series and eleven movies and counting. *Star Trek* was a watershed in television that made it possible for pointy-ear-wearing Trekkies to get laid by other nerds.

REASON: The space between every female alien's legs is a Captain Kirk's final frontier. His mission is to explore strange new civilizations and have sex with them. A penis with this nickname boldly goes where no man has gone before, and has no inhibitions when it comes to a girl's filthiest requests. Ladies, put on your sexiest blue masks and prepare for the Captain to board your ship!

RATING: 🍆

DEXTER

ORIGIN: The title character from the Showtime hit series appears to be a mild-mannered and sweet guy, but Dexter has a dark secret. Underneath his common-man exterior, Dexter is a serial killer who lives by a strict code: He only kills murderers, rapists, and other evil criminals who have gotten away with their misdeeds. Dexter's cover is a job as a blood spatter analyst with the Miami Police Department, working right under the noses of colleagues who would be shocked to know his true identity.

REASON: A man with a Dexter is a charming lady-killer with a creepy look in his eye. He is a sexy lover covering up a dark side, and the women he dates are always wondering what he's hiding, and why it turns them on so much.

RATING:

THE FRESH PRINCE

ORIGIN: As a young man Will Smith was a successful rapper who suddenly found himself owing millions of dollars to the IRS. The result was *The Fresh Prince of Bel-Air*, a sitcom built around Smith that was a convenient way for him to work his way out of debt, and along the way became a hit series.

REASON: A man with a Fresh Prince can charm anyone, anywhere, from the basketball courts of West Philadelphia to the mansions of Bel Air. To have a Fresh Prince, a man has to be street-smart, funny, and possibly accompanied by DJ Jazzy Jizz. Your parents won't understand your relationship, but after a summertime night of rapping you'll be unwrapping each other's clothes.

RATING:

GONZO

ORIGIN: Gonzo is a blue Muppet and renowned chicken aficionado with a long, hooked nose. For years it was never clear what species Gonzo actually is, until *Muppets from Space* revealed that he is part of an alien race. Gonzo has a crush on Miss Piggy, resulting in the only frog/pig/alien love-triangle in history.

REASON: A Gonzo dick is a rare find: a thick cock with a curve. Only the biggest dicks are so large that they have their own elbow. Its ability to get to those hard to reach spots inside you will send you into deep space.

RATING:

JACK TRIPPER

ORIGIN: *Three's Company* leading man Jack Tripper is one of TV's greatest characters of all time. He was the everyman that every man wished he could be. He was a lovable klutz who led a steady stream of beauties into his bed, while cunningly managing a gay façade to trick his landlord into letting him live with two hot-chick roommates.

REASON: A man with a Jack Tripper is a ladies' man who laughs in the face of squares, all the way to the bedroom. Ladies', come and knock on his door—and bring a friend.

RATING:

KENNY

ORIGIN: Kenny is a character from *South Park* whose filthy and perverted words are muffled by the bright orange snowsuit covering his mouth. Kenny gained notoriety in part because he was killed off in most episodes, only to reappear and die again in the following episode.

REASON: A guy with a Kenny can often be found in the North American mountain states, especially Colorado. He is recognizable by his hard-to-decipher dirty mouth and cheap winter clothes. An even rarer version will scream out "You killed Kenny!" post-orgasm. Yes, it can be disturbing.

RATING:

KNIGHT RIDER (AKA THE HOFF)

ORIGIN: The *Knight Rider* was David Hasselhoff's character Michael Knight, yet another mysterious eighties character that would travel the country solving crimes for no explainable reason. Knight Rider, however, had the advantage of driving a black corvette named Kit that was not only a genius, but had a cool English accent and a dry wit.

REASON: We're not exactly sure what the guy who possesses a Knight Rider actually looks like. Women may have hooked up with this guy numerous times but still don't know what color his hair is, let alone his eye color. A man with a Knight Rider likely meets women in a dark bar, makes love to them in a darkened bedroom, and is out the door before sunrise. He could be someone women encounter every day, like the barista at the local coffee shop or someone who works in a cubicle one floor below, but no one would ever know because no one has ever gotten a good look at him. He could even be a vampire, so it's probably best to avoid prying questions and just enjoy your evening rides.

RATING: 🍆

MACGYVER

ORIGIN: TV's MacGyver was a secret agent who used science and everyday objects to solve complicated problems. Stay in school kids, and you too can save the world!

REASON: A guy with a MacGyver has the ability to use his tool to unlock any box. If you wake up next to a computer programmer wondering how he so skillfully pulled off your skirt, you're with a MacGyver. Note: A MacGruber is a MacGyver's ineffective cousin.

RATING: /

MAGNUM P.I.

ORIGIN: *Magnum P.I.* was a hit show from the eighties starring Tom Selleck as a Vietnam vet turned private detective living in the mansion of a mysterious benefactor in Oahu, Hawaii. Each week Magnum would solve a case and bed a new beach babe.

REASON: Ferrari? Check. Beachfront Hawaiian estate? Check. Seventies-style porno stash? Check. Yes, a man with a Magnum P.I. has everything a lady could want, including the gun he keeps holstered in his tight jeans.

RATING: |

MR. BIG

ORIGIN: The HBO series *Sex and the City* was a rallying cry for all single women. After all, who needs a husband when there's a Mr. Big (played by Chris Noth) to play with? Note: Not to be confused with the corny eighties hair band that sang "To Be with You."

REASON: A man with a Mr. Big is so wealthy that his penis could open its own bank account. A serial philanderer, this guy is more likely to smoke a cigar while getting his "Mr. Big" smoked by an on-and-off again girlfriend than ever make a commitment. His motto — and a great line from the show: "Abso-fucking-lutely."

RATING: |

MR. FURLEY

ORIGIN: Don Knotts's comedic gifts are legendary, but his Mr. Furley character from *Three's Company* was seriously lacking in the sexiness department. Mr. Furley is the dream landlord, but despite his delusions of romantic grandeur, he is no dreamboat.

REASON: A Mr. Furley is what happens when a nerdy kid grows up without ever learning how to be cool. Men with Mr. Furleys will frequently latch on to younger, cooler guys in hope of scooping up some leftover ladies. This guy is lame, but a fashionable woman wouldn't mind borrowing one of his sassy scarves.

RATING:

MR. T

ORIGIN: Mr. T is a larger than life personality, more like an American mythic hero than an average man. Most people probably know him from the TV series *The A-Team*, where he appeared as the bruiser B. A. Baracus, whose catchphrase, "I pity the fool," became a pop-cultural phenomenon. Mr. T has also taken the form of a cartoon character, a professional wrestler, and a Hollywood Square.

REASON: Mr. T is big and badass, so a penis that is given this nom de plume must be equally impressive. He's best accompanied by a pubic hair Mohawk and a cock ring made of gold chains.

RATING:

PEE-WEE HERMAN

ORIGIN: *The Pee-wee Herman Show* was a wacky and surrealistic Saturday-morning series starring Paul Reubens. Pee-wee lived in a cartoon fantasy world come to life, surrounded by friends like a talking chair and a genie in a box.

REASON: Today's secret word is *tiny*! Try not to laugh too hard when you see this joker. This man-child of a member is more interested in his trike than a woman, and that "big adventure" won't be found with this guy.

RATING: 🌑

SPOCK

ORIGIN: *Star Trek's* biggest science geek may be superintelligent, but what he has in smarts he equally lacks in passion. Spock is half Vulcan, a race known for their pointy ears, neck pinches, and suppressing their emotions in favor of cold logic.

REASON: When someone with this dick gets excited all the blood rushes to the big brain in his head, not the little Spock in his pants. Vulcans are great to have around when you need help studying for your math test, but beam him up once you're ready to have some fun.

RATING: 🌑

TONY SOPRANO

ORIGIN: *The Sopranos* is HBO's portrayal of TV's most famous mafia family. It dramatically showed how the home life and the criminal life of New Jersey mobsters are messily mixed together.

REASON: Tony Soprano may have ended up in his psychiatrist's office for being a depressed sociopath prone to panic attacks, but all you need to care about is that in the bedroom (or kitchen, office, hotel, back of the Bada Bing) with one of his many goombahs he's always the big boss. A man with a Tony Soprano wakes up in the morning and finds himself a gun—*in his pants*.

RATING: 🖊

Literary Names

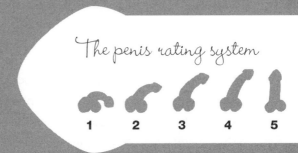

The penis rating system

1 2 3 4 5

There's nothing like curling up with a good book, but it's even better to curl up with a good cock. After all, a book may make you smarter, but a dick will keep you warm and will tucker you out so you have a sound sleep. That's why nine out of ten librarians recommend you bookend your day with a penis you love. So check out this chapter of literary-inspired names and then put this book down so you can name the characters in your own love story.

AHAB

ORIGIN: Ahab is the name of the doomed sea captain from *Moby Dick* who is obsessed with killing the eponymous white whale. Moby Dick destroyed one of Ahab's legs during a previous expedition, but Ahab didn't appreciate the gift of a brand-new peg leg and was determined to hunt the whale down no matter what the cost. Ahab and his crew paid for his fixation with their lives.

REASON: A guy with an Ahab is searching for the perfect "10." He will look far and wide for the ideal mate, feeling in his gut that his "white whale" is just around the corner. If a woman happens to pass his rigorous tests for a hook-up he'll initially make her feel extra-special, but will inevitably find a problem with her and toss her back into the sea. His delusional standards will turn him into the old man at the end of the bar telling stories to no one in particular about the one that got away.

RATING:

ALADDIN

ORIGIN: Aladdin is a character from a medieval Middle Eastern folktale. His story was popularized throughout the Western world in translations of *One Thousand and One Nights* in the eighteenth century, and more recently in an animated Disney film. Aladdin begins the story as a troublemaker duped into helping an evil sorcerer, but he gains the upper hand and fabulous riches with the help of a genie in a magic lamp.

REASON: A man with an Aladdin is a handsome and dark fellow who wants to take a woman for a spin on his magic carpet. When he rubs a lady like a lamp, she'll want to grant his every wish.

RATING:

THE BEAST

ORIGIN: *Beauty and the Beast* is a beloved fairy tale that has been perennially adapted and retold. In essence, the story is about a handsome and good man who is magically transformed into a beast and the beautiful girl who sees past his monstrous looks and falls for the man inside.

REASON: A man endowed with the Beast isn't cute like a Disney cartoon and he definitely doesn't sing musical numbers; he's a wild and woolly man-imal, and that's just how ladies like him. Parents and friends may warn women to stay away from the Beast, but that's because they don't know the real person inside his frightening exterior. However, his lover sees his inner beauty—and relishes the feel of the Beast between her thighs.

RATING:

BILBO BAGGINS

ORIGIN: Before Frodo came along, Bilbo was the original celebrity Hobbit. He first appeared in J. R. R. Tolkien's *The Hobbit* and was seen again in *The Lord of the Rings* trilogy, and later was portrayed by Ian Holm in the live-action trilogy. Bilbo is small, but his courage is a lot bigger than his height.

REASON: Nothing against short guys in general, but there is a certain kind of smaller guy, known as the Hobbit type, who has a Bilbo Baggins in his pants that's positively dwarfish compared to that of other men. Complicating matters is the fact that he tries to compensate for his short stature by being overly bold in the bedroom, stopping at nothing to get inside a woman's "precious." Sorry Bilbo, over-eager meager-sized men are not attractive.

RATING:

CASANOVA

ORIGIN: Casanova was a real man born in Venice, Italy, in 1725 who spent his life traveling the world and mixing it up with the rich and famous. He made his name by seducing and sleeping with every woman he could find, and we get to read about his saucy adventures in *Histoire de ma vie*, his autobiography.

REASON: A man with a true Casanova is sexy, romantic, and has an irresistible Italian accent. A Casanova has seduced women around the world and he's always looking for another conquest to add to his ever-growing list. This dick will scandalize every woman he meets and they won't regret a second of it.

RATING:

DON JUAN

ORIGIN: The character Don Juan comes from a Spanish legend first published in the seventeenth century, but he was a folk hero long before that. You've got to give it to the Spanish when it comes to folk heroes. They look up to a guy who is famous for all the sex he had, while the Americans ended up with a guy who just planted a bunch of apple trees.

REASON: Literature's greatest lover is a libertine famous for being a womanizer; no wonder he's been portrayed by Johnny Depp on film. A man with a Don Juan for a dick will wine, dine, and 1669 his lover without hesitation. He lulls his loves with poetry and kisses, and ladies should feel free to let him seduce them, but they shouldn't be naive. After all, he isn't whispering sweet nothings to just one woman.

RATING:

DR. JEKYLL AND MR. HYDE

ORIGIN: In the novel *The Strange Case of Dr Jekyll and Mr. Hyde*, by Robert Louis Stevenson, the civilized Dr. Jekyll creates a potion that changes him into the despicable Mr. Hyde. Hyde is the physical expression of Jekyll's dark side, a pleasure-seeking and cruel villain.

REASON: We've all met this kind of split personality: a nice guy who gets a few drinks of "potion" in him and turns into a complete jerk. If a woman ends up with a guy with a Dr. Jekyll and Mr. Hyde she should feel free to throw some of her own potion right in his face. This is also a good name for the cock of a guy who appears to be a stud, but drinks too much and disappoints his lady friend with whiskey-dick when she want to get frisky.

RATING:

FAUST

ORIGIN: Faust is a tragic character from early German folklore. His story, in which he trades his soul to the Devil in exchange for knowledge and power, has been retold for centuries. Faust's warning about unchecked pride has inspired dozens of playwrights, novelists, and musicians—probably because people always need to be scared into doing the right thing.

REASON: Faust gets this name because only someone who's made a deal with the devil could have a penis this perfect. But he's too good to be true. Sadly, your relationship with Faust will end badly, but you'll have a hell of a good time until it goes up in flames.

RATING:

HANNIBAL LECTER

ORIGIN: Hannibal Lecter is a genius, psychiatrist, and sociopathic cannibal who first appeared in a series of novels by Thomas Harris. He was immortalized in most people's minds in horrifying fashion by Anthony Hopkins's Oscar-winning portrayal in the 1991 film *The Silence of the Lambs*.

REASON: Lecter is one of the world's most terrifying villains, so it's a good nickname for an ex's penis. When a woman first meets this penis, it mesmerizes her. But later, she may have to see a shrink to deal with the scary nightmares of this evil penis gobbling her up.

RATING:

JACK

ORIGIN: *Jack and the Beanstalk* is a popular English fairy tale that has been told in various forms for hundreds of years. The version that is most commonly told today starts with a poor young man named Jack who trades his family's last cow for some magic beans. The beans grow into a huge stalk that leads Jack to an evil giant's home in the clouds, where Jack robs the giant blind of his magical valuables and ends up killing him. Jack was a thief and a murderer, but giant-cide wasn't illegal back in those days, so he lived guilt-free and happily ever after.

REASON: Jack can be used as a generic name for any stud you keep in your stable, but it is more commonly used as the name of the dick of an older guy who needs "magic beans" to make his "stalk" grow. Without his beans Jack is average size, but once he's got some magic in him he turns into a giant and starts looking for hens to lay.

RATING:

LANCELOT

ORIGIN: Lancelot first appeared in print in Chrétien de Troyes's medieval tale *Le Chevalier de la charrette*. Lancelot is one of the Knights of the Round Table, well known for his search for the Holy Grail and for having an affair with King Arthur's wife, Guinevere.

REASON: Most guys wouldn't want the slippery Lancelot visiting their house while they're out of town, but a woman like Guinevere will be happily swept off her feet and right into Lancelot's bed. Lance knows how to please a woman. After all, he is named after an enormously long weapon for a good reason.

RATING:

MERLIN

ORIGIN: The legendary figure Merlin has appeared in stories for over a thousand years. He's most commonly associated with the Arthurian legend of the Knights of the Round Table in his role as an advisor and sorcerer.

REASON: He isn't a knight in shining armor, but a man with a modern-day Merlin has the power to put a woman under his spell. He may have a few gray hairs in his "beard," but he can make clothes magically disappear with a wave of this magic wand.

RATING:

THE PIED PIPER

ORIGIN: The legend of the Pied Piper takes place long ago in the town of Hamelin, which was suffering from a rat infestation. A piper in multicolored (pied) clothing appeared in Hamelin and said that for a price he could use his music to rid the town of its rats. The man did as he promised, but when it came time to pay the piper, the townspeople reneged on the deal, and the piper swore revenge. The piper returned, and this time used his magical music to lead all the children of Hamelin out of town, never to be seen again.

REASON: These days a man with a Pied Piper probably won't be playing a pipe; he's more likely a wannabe DJ or a guy with an acoustic guitar who will use his limited musical talents to put a woman under his spell—before he leads her to his bed. Ladies, if you fall for the Piper, just be aware that you aren't the first to fall for his hypnotic music.

RATING:

PINOCCHIO

ORIGIN: Pinocchio first appeared in a nineteenth-century Italian novel, *The Adventures of Pinocchio*. It was one of the world's first pieces of children's literature and was the inspiration for the classic Disney animated film *Pinocchio*, which premiered in 1940. The original story was much darker than later versions and described a much harsher resolution for the disobedient wooden boy whose nose grows longer with every lie he tells.

REASON: Women may wish that the Pinocchio story were real and that every guy's member would grow longer from lying, because every guy they met would be hung like a log. As it stands, Pinocchio is a name for a penis whose size is dependent on the "lies" of those enhancement treatments seen on late-night infomercials.

RATING:

ROMEO

ORIGIN: Shakespeare's tragic hero Romeo in his play *Romeo and Juliet* was destined to die in the arms of his girlfriend, Juliet. Ever since Romeo first took his life over his lost love, Emo teens have been threatening to slit their wrists over their dramatic love lives.

REASON: A man with a Romeo is first and foremost a great lover who knows how to please his lady—even though the relationship will likely end with a tragic, but bloodless, breakup.

RATING:

RUMPELSTILTSKIN (AKA RUMPLEFORESKIN)

ORIGIN: Rumpelstiltskin first appeared in *Children's and Household Tales*, by the Brothers Grimm in 1812. He is a scheming dwarf who helps an imprisoned maiden spin straw into gold—for a price. They cut a deal whereby she promises him her firstborn child. This mysteri-

ous manipulator's secret name was the key to rescuing the baby.

REASON: Nowadays the name Rumpelstiltskin is synonymous with penises of creepy, needy, diminutive guys who go for single MILFs. These penises think that single moms are vulnerable and therefore susceptible to its advances. Ladies, don't let this dick trick you into thinking that he's anything more than a creepy wiener who's trying to hide his true identity.

RATING:

TARZAN

ORIGIN: In the novel *Tarzan of the Apes*, Tarzan is the son of English aristocrats whose ship was marooned on the coast of Africa when he was still a baby. His parents died, so naturally, a tribe of apes raised him. Tarzan's story is kind of like the plot of the movie *The Blue Lagoon*, but instead of being marooned with a teenage Brooke Shields he was stuck with a bunch of gorillas. However, he did attain superhuman strength, could swing from the trees, and learned to talk to animals.

REASON: A man with a Tarzan communicates better with a dog than with a woman, but that's not a bad tradeoff if she ends up swinging from her four-poster when in bed with her wild beast-man.

RATING:

Monster Names

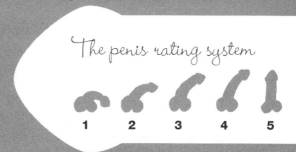

The penis rating system

1   2   3   4   5

Whether they come from the black lagoon or from another planet, everyone loves being frightened by these monstrous cocks. Of course, some penises are just plain scary and need to be driven off by an angry mob of torch-bearing villagers. You'll find the appropriate names for these big, scary, out of control dicks in this chapter.

BOGEYMAN

ORIGIN: Look under your bed! Parents from cultures around the world tell their children tales of a ghostlike monster that will "get them" if they don't behave. In America this figure is often referred to as the Bogeyman and it's often said that he lives in the dark corners of a child's room at night.

REASON: Unfortunately your parents were right that there are real Bogeyman, but they aren't ghosts or goblins. A Bogeyman belongs to a guy who attempts a late-night booty call by showing up unannounced looking for nooky. Ladies, don't open the door or the Bogeyman will get you!

RATING:

CHUPACABRA

ORIGIN: It seems like every monster is hundreds of years old, but there is at least one beastie that has much more recent origins. The Chupacabra has only started appearing in Latin American countries over the last couple decades. Confounded farmers report of a frightening "goat sucker" that terrorizes farm animals south of the border, sucking them dry of blood in the middle of the night.

REASON: Chupacabra is the perfect name for a sexy Latino penis that belongs to a man who loves to suck on his lady all through the hot and steamy night. Buenas noches!

RATING:

COCKATRICE

ORIGIN: From a medieval English legend, the cockatrice is a creature that resembles a rooster with a large, lizard-like tail and has the Medusa-like power to turn someone to stone with just a glance. Legend has it that a cockatrice is born from an egg laid by a cock and incubated by a toad. So keep your cocks and toads in separate cages to prevent genetic monsters from being born.

REASON: A Cockatrice is so awful looking we can't tell if it's human, animal, or some horrible combination of the two. A cock like this is ugly as a toad and should be avoided. If you do see one, whatever you do don't stare at it too long or it may turn you to stone.

RATING:

DRACULA

ORIGIN: The gothic novel *Dracula*, by Bram Stoker, was inspired by Vlad the Impaler, a Transylvanian prince infamous for the cruel treatment of his enemies. His subjects referred to him as Dracula, which means "son of the dragon" in Latin.

REASON: Vampires used to get a bad rap, but not anymore. They are now in vogue, and why shouldn't they be? A man with a Dracula loves to suck, suck, suck the blood of his victim. Yes, a Dracula dick likes to have sex during that time of the month. So if you're a woman who isn't scared of a vampire dipping his fang into your blood supply, just let him go with the flow.

RATING:

FRANKENSTEIN

ORIGIN: Dr. Frankenstein's monster was an unnatural creation, brought to life by questionable scientific methods. The monster was large and he was hideous. He horrified his maker—and everyone else who laid eyes on him. The monster suffered for his creator's hubris and, in the end, he returns the favor and ruins the life of his maker.

REASON: Like Dr. Frankenstein's monster, a Frankenstein dick is an unauthentic monstrosity, brought to life through pills, herbal enhancements, and surgery to make it bigger. This Franken-footer is really a Frankenweenie. Grab your torch and scare it away!

RATING:

GODZILLA

ORIGIN: Godzilla is Japan's monstrous export who infamously knocked down buildings with a sweep of his tail. Godzilla represented Japanese fears of another nuclear attack and preoccupied the country's consciousness until they got a new obsession: robots.

REASON: A Godzilla dick is so big it will sweep the lamp off the night table when the guy attached to this huge cock gets out of bed. Be prepared by putting all valuables in a drawer and putting the cap back on the bottle of lube after each use.

RATING:

GOLEM

ORIGIN: A golem is an automaton constructed from inanimate materials to look humanlike and then brought to life by supernatural means. The most famous golem tale is of the Prague Golem, who was created by a sixteenth-century rabbi to protect the city's Jews from attack.

REASON: In modern Hebrew, golem is the word for "rock," so this is a good name for a hard-as-stone Jewish penis that keeps you safe and stimulated. His owner will also be a good boy and introduce you to his mother the next day.

RATING:

KING KONG

ORIGIN: King Kong made his first appearance as the title character in the 1933 film. He is the most misunderstood monster in history. All he wanted was some alone time with a cute blond. Instead he was unfairly kidnapped from his home and taken to New York City to be put on display.

REASON: A man with a King Kong is a proud ape who will break his shackles and sacrifice himself in order to protect his lady. His ability to stomp through a woman's subconscious, teasing her with fantasies of monkey love, is unparalleled and drives that lucky lady's desire for well-hung guys.

RATING:

THE MUMMY

ORIGIN: When an ancient Egyptian pharaoh died his body was preserved through the process of mummification: The organs were removed and the body was dehydrated, wrapped in linen, and buried underground. Egyptians believed the process would grant eternal life to their rulers. Today there is a similar mummification process, but we call it Botox.

REASON: A trouser Mummy is similarly old and dried up, but one thing's for sure—this stiff won't live forever. Ladies, if you meet one, be sure to wrap it up in latex "bandages" before you bury it inside your pyramid. But we recommend that you stay away, or you may be punished with a curse.

RATING:

NESSIE (AKA LOCH NESS MONSTER)

ORIGIN: People have been reporting sightings of a great beast that lives in the waters of Scotland's Loch Ness for centuries. The dragonlike creature is rumored to be a descendant of the dinosaurs. It gained worldwide fame when a picture was taken that supposedly proved that a large creature with a neck thicker than an elephant's trunk was living in the lake. That picture has been proven false, but true believers will never accept something like "evidence."

REASON: No one can prove the existence of the Loch Ness monster, but there is evidence of "elephant necked" sea-monsters that prefer sex in the water. Nessies hide in bathing suits and make an appearance when a sexy lass slips into the pool.

RATING:

PREDATOR

ORIGIN: *The Predator* is an alien that invaded movie theaters in 1987 in order to hunt down a group of soldiers made up of 1980s heroes and future governors Arnold Schwarzenegger and Jesse Ventura. The Governator eventually defeated Predator, but the Predator left its mark as one of sci-fi's great warriors.

REASON: A notable characteristic of the Predator, which is revealed whenever it takes off its mask, is that it's ugly as sin. In this case, beauty and brawn do not go together. Likewise, a Predator prick is powerful and worth a tussle, but it won't win any beauty contests.

RATING:

SASQUATCH (AKA BIGFOOT)

ORIGIN: For centuries, Native American tribes have told stories of a giant apelike creature stalking the forests of the Pacific Northwest. Later frontiersmen and settlers in the region began telling similar tales of a hairy beastman living in the woods. Bigfoot is rarely seen, but occasionally a huge unidentifiable footprint will appear, stoking the legend of the Sasquatch.

REASON: The legend of Bigfoot is the inspiration for the Sasquatch penis: a dick rumored to be so large that it's hard to believe it belongs to a human. The proof of its existence is minimal; the only evidence is an occasional imprint stamped on an ass. Is Sasquatch real, or is it an elaborate hoax? Only a really lucky lady will have the opportunity to uncover the truth.

RATING:

Mythological Names

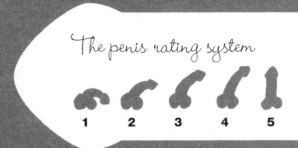

The penis rating system

1   2   3   4   5

Back in the day, people didn't have TVs and movies, so they told each other myths and legends about their gods and heroes. Many of these stories were so graphically violent and sexual that they were the ancient equivalent of Cinemax's adult programming. The Greek, Norse, and Roman gods were either beating each other up or having sex with everything in sight (especially the Greek gods, who were horny beyond belief). Lots of myths recite the gods' exploits as they boned their way across the world cheating on their wives and scandalizing virgins as they spread their seed. These myths were ostensibly used to explain the origin of things like plants and animals, but they were also a handy excuse to tell some hot, sexy stories. They also provided a nice explanation as to why men are always thinking with their dicks. After all, when a society's omnipotent creators are irascible perverts, how can humans expect to control themselves? Find inspiration in these classic names from myth and legend.

ACHILLES

ORIGIN: Achilles is the central hero of the Trojan War and was the Greek's best warrior. He was super-humanly strong and nearly invulnerable, except for a weakness in one spot—his heel.

REASON: A blow to Achilles' heel caused his death; therefore, this is an appropriate name for a big, strong cock that has a flaw. Maybe the guy has a big dick but can't get it up? The name Achilles can also be used for the penis of a guy who has a sex addiction, or one who always falls for the wrong girl.

RATING:

AJAX

ORIGIN: Along with Achilles, Ajax was one of the greatest and most famous Greek warriors of the Trojan War. He was a big, strong, and fierce warrior who commanded an army without suffering any wounds in battle.

REASON: Ajax's weapon of choice was a long spear, so this is a good name for a guy who's armed with a hefty weapon. The Ajax penis can fly across the room and pin a lucky lady to the bed. Impressive yes, but don't forget to put on a Trojan before going in to battle.

RATING:

ATLAS

ORIGIN: Greek mythology says that Atlas was a Titan who fought and lost against Zeus in a primordial war. As punishment, his duty is now to hold up the world and keep the sky from crashing into the earth. Let's all hope that Atlas's back doesn't give out.

REASON: The name Atlas goes to a penis that is strong enough to hold a lady astride and spin her like a globe without dropping her. A guy with this dick is a huge fan of big butts, because he loves to hold on to two round globes.

RATING:

CYCLOPS

ORIGIN: The Cyclopes are a race of giants from Greek myth, distinctively marked by a single eye in the middle of their forehead. In one story a Cyclops captured the Greek hero Odysseus, who escaped the clutches of the giant by putting out the Cyclops's eye with a spear.

REASON: This name is appropriate for any penis, because every dick resembles a one-eyed monster. However, Cyclops is a fantastic name for a penis with a particularly large and scary pee-hole.

RATING:

DIONYSUS (GREEK) OR BACCHUS (ROMAN)

ORIGIN: Dionysus oversees the good stuff in life, like wine and ecstatic madness. Simply put, he is the god of partying. He travels the world, surrounded by drunken nymphs and horny satyrs who play music, dance, and have orgies. If he were worshipped today, he'd be the patron god of Las Vegas.

REASON: A penis named Dionysus delivers lots of sex and fun but it comes with a price. Ladies, if you spend the night with a Dionysus he'll party your pants off, but you'll wakeup with a hangover.

RATING:

GILGAMESH

ORIGIN: The Mesopotamian poem about the hero Gilgamesh is one of the world's earliest epics. Okay, Gilgamesh is an odd name, but the guy was a demigod, not to mention king of Babylon, so give it some respect. Gilgamesh wasn't just a ridiculously powerful god-king; he was a prideful and passionate man who discovers his humanity at the end of his story through love.

REASON: A Gilgamesh cock belongs to a guy who starts pursuing a woman with only the intention of getting her into bed, but has a change of heart after going through an epic struggle to attain her. This penis finds out after a long journey that he not only loves his pussy, but that he's in love with his pussy as well.

RATING:

HERCULES

ORIGIN: Hercules is probably the most famous warrior from ancient Greek mythology. He battled beasts and monsters in order to make the world safe for mankind, so you might say he was the world's first superhero. Hercules's most well-known tale was of the twelve labors that he had to complete for Hera, the queen of the gods.

REASON: A Hercules penis loves nothing more than a challenge, so an easy sexual conquest won't get this love muscle to flex. This dick only gets hard when a girl plays hard to get.

RATING:

LOKI

ORIGIN: The Norse god Loki was a troublemaker, liar, and trickster. He also used magic and shape shifting in his nefarious schemes. He caused problems for the gods, especially Thor, whom he envied.

REASON: A Loki is a dick that gets off on getting into crazy situations, like streaking across a college campus, or having a threesome in an airplane bathroom, because it's all just a big laugh. When this penis gets into trouble, he shifts shape from a little jester into a big joker.

RATING:

MEDUSA

ORIGIN: Medusa is Greek mythology's best-known Gorgon, a female monster whose hair was a mass of living snakes. One look at Medusa's ugly mug would turn the gazer into stone. Her cave was decorated with the frozen statues of warriors who had attempted to kill her. Medusa was finally done in by Perseus, who chopped off her head and gave it to the goddess Athena as a gift.

REASON: A Medusa is topped with an unkempt, overgrown mass of curly pubes that will freeze your face in a state of shock. A man with a Medusa has only two options: he

can chop off that nest of snakes or he can stay dateless in his man-cave.

RATING:

MIDAS

ORIGIN: Midas was a king in Greek mythology who was granted one wish by the gods. Thinking he was outsmarting them, Midas wished that all he touched would turn to gold. He was granted the wish, but soon regretted it when everything he touched turned to gold. The gods eventually reversed the curse, but in a later story Midas pissed off the god Apollo, who punished him by giving him donkey's ears for being so stupid.

REASON: The moniker Midas can be used to refer to a rich dick or a stupid dumbass. A guy who has a Midas dick is so smug he thinks that everything his penis touches will turn to gold (figuratively speaking). But this guy is peddling fool's gold; a Midas is nothing but a cheap imitation.

RATING:

ODIN

ORIGIN: Odin was the king of the Norse gods who were worshipped by the tribes of Germany and, later, the Vikings. Hordes of warriors fought their way across Europe, conquering, pillaging, and eventually overrunning the Roman Empire, all in the name of Odin. Fun fact for trivia buffs: Wednesday is named after Woden, the English form of Odin.

REASON: Women should let their man conquer and pillage his way across their bodies in the name of his godlike penis, Odin. This Viking of a dick might have a ginger beard like Eric the Red or be like Leif Eric-

son and explore some lucky lady's coastline. Odin is a bit of a savage, but he's a king among penises.

RATING:

POSEIDON

ORIGIN: Poseidon is one of the major gods of Greek myth. According to the *Iliad*, back when the world was divided up among the gods, Poseidon got the sea. Sailors and fisherman worshipped him in hope of safe return to land.

REASON: A Poseidon is a dick that loves to have sex on a boat. Frequently seen during spring break or summer vacation, a guy with a Poseidon can often be found cruising a Royal Caribbean ship looking for single ladies to be his first mate.

RATING:

THOR

ORIGIN: Thor is the god of thunder according to Norse mythology. He was a highly revered god in Viking myth, and later with comic-book fans. Thor's weapon of choice was his hammer, which he used to rain down thunder and lightning. Onscreen you can see sexy thunder-pants in a cameo in the 1987 female-favorite movie *Adventures in Babysitting*.

REASON: Getting hammered by Thor is like being shocked by electricity and rocked by thunder at the same time. He'll blast any woman straight to thunder-cloud nine.

RATING:

TITAN

ORIGIN: In Greek mythology the Titans are a race of old-time gods who ruled the world before Zeus and the other Olympians took over.

They were locked up and punished for eternity for their aggressiveness, and nowadays they only make occasional appearances in movie titles that start with *Remember the . . .* or *Clash of the. . . .*

REASON: A man with a Titanic-sized penis is worthy of this name. Titans also like it rough, so they don't mind being bound and slapped around all in the name of fun.

RATING:

ZEUS

ORIGIN: Zeus is the head honcho, the king of the Greek gods. As the lord of the sky and thunder, Zeus can control the weather and rain down bolts of lightning as he sees fit. He's also well known for bedding down every nymph and pretty girl he sees, despite being married to Hera.

REASON: Zeus is a penis that needs a condom to contain his powerful "lightning bolts." So unless a woman wants little Aphrodites and Hercules running around, she had better use birth control when being wooed by a guy who claims he's got the Sky King in his shorts.

RATING:

Religious Names

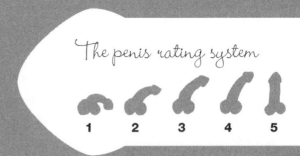

The penis rating system

1 2 3 4 5

Great sex is usually accompanied by yelps of "Oh my God!" and can feel like a holy ritual. The Hindus literally wrote the book on sex, the *Kamasutra*, and the Judeo-Christian faiths command us all to be fruitful and multiply, so it makes sense to find a name among the world's religions. So bow your head and say a little prayer as we open up the holy robes and take a look at some religious names.

BIBLICAL NAMES

Penis naming goes back to the beginning. It's right there in the opening of the Old Testament: After creating every creature on Earth, God gives each one a name. Man became Adam. Woman became Eve. And that long, slithering thing? It became the serpent. Now, some people read the Bible literally and assume a snake is just a snake. But perhaps the "serpent" was actually a nickname for Adam's organ. God created everything else, so it's only logical that he invented the world's first nickname for the world's first penis, no? Let's look at the evidence:

- The Serpent was a trickster who got Eve into a world of trouble.
- He lied to Eve, probably so he could watch her wrap her lips around that juicy apple. *Mmmm*.
- Ever since that moment in Eden, women have been both intrigued and frightened by snakes.

That sure sounds like a penis. In fact, it seems pretty obvious that God wasn't talking about a real reptile. Instead, he was acting like a good dad, warning Eve about her new boyfriend and the consequences that come with sex. God was probably just embarrassed to say "penis" during the heart to heart with his daughter, so he used a euphemism (*serpent*) instead, and the name stuck. Like a lot of girls, Eve learned her lesson the hard way and ended up getting kicked out of Eden. Yes, she lost paradise, but she discovered how much fun it was to play with Adam's trouser snake. The following list of biblical names will be like taking a bite of the apple of knowledge and will help you discover a blessed penis name.

BEHEMOTH

ORIGIN: The Book of Job describes the Behemoth as the largest animal to ever roam Earth. The Behemoth's limbs are like copper, his bones are like iron, and his tail is as hard as cedar. Prophets foretold that Leviathan and Behemoth would fight to the death during Armageddon.

REASON: A Behemoth cock is a one in a million penis, so if you find one stay in bed and enjoy it even if it's the end of the world outside. We also suggest you find a Leviathan and a Behemoth to fight over you in bed.

RATING:

DANIEL

ORIGIN: In the Book of Daniel, the Babylonian king Nebuchadnezzar captures our courageous hero. Most of the king's captives don't live for long, but Daniel survives by accurately interpreting the king's dreams. Daniel's psychic powers allowed him to see the future, but unfortunately he did not foresee the king turning on him and throwing him into a den of lions. Amazingly, Danny's magical skills gave him the power to survive a night among the lions without a single cat-scratch on him.

REASON: A dreamy guy with a Daniel isn't afraid of a lion's den, known in our modern times as a bar full of hungry cougars. He can often be found picking up sophisticated older women in areas like Aspen and Orange County. A hot, mature hellcat might choose to affectionately nickname her lover's cock "Danny Boy."

RATING:

DAVID

ORIGIN: David was an ancient king who became an important figure in Judaism, Christianity, and Islam. When he was just a boy he became the original underdog (see the following Goliath entry). Before the fight with Goliath, David bravely refused armor from the Israelite king himself and chose to go into battle with just his shepherd's staff and a sling. When he grew up, David became the king of Israel and was much loved by his people, despite the fact that he was less than perfect. He had multiple wives, was guilty of adultery, and on several occasions, he dealt with his problems by killing people. But mostly we remember his staggering courage.

REASON: He might not be the biggest guy around, but a guy with a David is surprisingly powerful. After all, he killed a giant and became king, so a woman should be proud to hold this scepter.

RATING:

GOLIATH

ORIGIN: Goliath first appeared in the Old Testament in the story of his "gigantic" battle with David, the future king of Israel (see the previous "David" entry). As you may have heard, the fight didn't go so well for Goliath. He was the biggest and strongest warrior of the Philistines, who were fighting the Israelites. Goliath boldly challenged the Israelites to send out a single warrior to fight him in man-to-man combat. Only the boy David was brave enough to accept Goliath's challenge. The Philistines were confident that their man would win, but David shocked everybody by conquering

Goliath with a single shot from his sling.

REASON: Before David made him famous, Goliath was the original jock. Despite his eventual downfall, he was big, strong, and infamous for delivering mighty wedgies unto the nerdy Israelites. A man with a Goliath in his loincloth is a giant stud who falls (in love possibly?) all too easily.

RATING: 🍆

JESUS

ORIGIN: Jesus Christ is the central figure of Christianity, believed by Christians to be the Messiah and the Son of God. Jesus' popularity with his followers was considered a threat to the ruling Roman government, so he was put to death by crucifixion. According to the Bible, Jesus rose from the dead three days later and ascended to Heaven, and today billions of people honor his

sacrifice with Christmas gifts and Easter egg hunts.

REASON: If you hear or say "Oh my God!" when the pants drop, then you have a Jesus on your hands. If you're a lady, kneel down, open your mouth for communion, and get ready for a religious experience. If you're a man, just say to yourself, "Hallelujah! God is good!"

RATING: 🍆

JONAH

ORIGIN: Jonah was a prophet in the Bible who was swallowed by a great fish while at sea. He spent three days and three nights inside the belly of the fish until God had it spit him out.

REASON: A man with a Jonah is a chubby chaser who is often overpowered by the women he courts. We respect that this dick is into larger ladies, but he isn't very discriminating about the quality of the women he's interested in. He probably has low self-esteem, because he ends up with a woman who beats him down—plus, he usually smells like fish.

RATING:

JUDAS

ORIGIN: Judas Iscariot was one of Jesus Christ's twelve apostles, but he is best known for his betrayals. Judas identified Jesus to the Roman soldiers by giving him a kiss on the cheek after the Last Supper and basically signed Jesus' death warrant. After Christ's execution, Judas was so distraught that he hanged himself. The name Judas has become synonymous with betrayal, and the theme of a traitor's "Judas kiss" is a favorite among musicians ranging from U2 to Metallica and Judas Priest.

REASON: Beware of this penis! He'll act like your best friend, and may even give you a kiss . . . right until he stabs you in your backside.

RATING:

LEVIATHAN

ORIGIN: According to the Old Testament, Leviathan was a huge sea monster made by God on the fifth day of Creation. Legend has it that he is three hundred miles long and resides in the Mediterranean Sea. Later writers used Leviathan as a metaphor for Satan, which seems appropriate given all the sailors who have drowned at sea.

REASON: It takes a mighty member to be named after the Bible's biggest sea monster. If you're lucky enough to possess or make love to a Leviathan, hold on tight and prepare for the bed to get very wet.

RATING:

METHUSELAH

ORIGIN: Methuselah was Noah's grandfather—and the oldest living man in the Bible. He is said to have been 969 years old when he died.

REASON: Methuselah is a good fit for a penis belonging to any sexy senior. Old he may be, but with age comes lots of experience and knowledge of ancient sexual positions.

RATING:

MOSES

ORIGIN: Moses was a Jew born in Egypt at a time when the pharaoh had ordered the murder of all Jewish boys. To save him, his mother sent him down the Nile in a reed basket, where he was found and adopted by the pharaoh's daughter. Despite being raised as Egyptian royalty, Moses learned of his roots and eventually became the savior of the Jewish people, freeing them from bondage in Egypt. He also had a direct line to God via the Bible's version of the cell phone, a flaming bush.

REASON: Moses parts legs like he parted the Red Sea, and he's not afraid of a woman's monthly "plague." He is also rumored to have a direct line to God, especially when a redheaded lady love flashes her flaming bush.

RATING:

NOAH

ORIGIN: Judaism, Christianity, and Islam all tell the story of the great flood that God sent to punish mankind for its wickedness. Noah was the only good man left, so God chose him to build a ship and gather all the creatures of the earth, two-by-two, aboard it. Noah, along with his family and the animals, survived the flood and eventually repopulated the world.

REASON: This holy sailor takes his ladies two at a time, so you'd better bring a raincoat, 'cause there'll be no dry land in sight. But beware: A man with a Noah has a thing for furries (two at a time).

RATING:

SAMSON

ORIGIN: Samson was a superhero of the Old Testament, blessed with unbelievable strength. It is said that Samson wrestled a lion and slew an entire army with the jawbone of a donkey. However, Samson's girlfriend, Delilah, betrayed him by cutting off his hair—the source of his strength—thus making him vulnerable to capture by the Philistines.

REASON: Samson is a mighty strong boy, but he's way too proud of his bushy pubes. But, his self-confidence comes from his "lion's mane," and he needs to be compli-

mented on it to be happy. However, any woman who names her man "Samson" probably ought not to be trusted—be wary of any "I shave you/you shave me" games, guys.

RATING:

SATAN (AKA LUCIFER)

ORIGIN: He goes by different names, but no matter what you choose to call him, this guy's the Devil. In the Old Testament Satan made a wager with God over the soul of Job. Later in the New Testament, Lucifer is said to have once been God's favorite angel but was then cast out of heaven for the sin of pride. Satan then became the embodiment and perpetrator of temptation and evil on Earth as well as the overseer of Hell.

REASON: He may have been an innocent angel once, but now Satan is guaranteed to get a woman into trouble. But she'll have fun on the road to ruin, so she should sit back and enjoy the ride. Beware of horns and red skin. Yikes!

RATING: /

ZIZ

ORIGIN: The third great beast mentioned in the Old Testament was Ziz, who ruled the sky. The ancient Hebrews said that Ziz was a birdlike creature whose wingspan was large enough to block out the sun. Due to his size and physical prowess, Ziz was charged with protecting all the world's birds.

REASON: The modern-day Ziz is a big penis with a big heart who will always take care of his "chick." Ladies, we recommend you stay in and nest with a Ziz.

RATING: /

BUDDHISM AND HINDUISM

Eastern philosophies teach us that good karma will lead to good sex. Well, maybe that's not a strict interpretation of Buddhism and Hinduism, but it's not too far off to believe that the religions that introduced the world to Nirvana, tantric sex, and the *Kamasutra* believe in a healthy sex life. The following Eastern-inspired names are a good fit for a penis that wishes to shed itself of earthly suffering and be reincarnated as a sex god.

BUDDHA

ORIGIN: The founder of Buddhism was an Indian prince who lived a sheltered life until he learned of all the suffering in the world. He chose to give up his possessions and power and seek enlightenment in order to become Buddha, "the enlightened one."

REASON: Buddha will teach you things that will bring you to a new plane of sexual existence. He is a specialist in night-long tantric sex.

RATING:

SHIVA

ORIGIN: One of the principal Hindu gods who oversees the universe, Shiva's eternal dance represents ends and beginnings—that is, the cycle of life. So yeah, that's a pretty awesome name for a penis.

REASON: Shiva is also the god of yoga, so the name best fits a guy who can twist into a pretzel in order to keep those orgasms coming and coming in a nightly cycle.

RATING:

VISHNU

ORIGIN: Many Hindus regard Vishnu as the supreme god and preserver of the universe. He is often depicted as having dark-blue skin and four arms, which represent his massive power.

REASON: This is a dick that seems to know just what you need, as though he's omniscient. Vishnu is so skilled in the sexual arts that it will feel as though he has four hands that are everywhere at once. Go ahead and let those "hands" roam.

RATING:

Cosmic Names

The penis rating system

1 2 3 4 5

The constellations have been used to predict the destiny of human-kind for millennia, so we predict that time spent with a penis deserving of a name from the stars will be an otherworldly experience. Grab hold of these pocket rockets and blast off into orbit. The spacey names in this chapter are right for the penis that's located at the center of your universe.

BIG BANG

ORIGIN: The Big Bang is the event that created our universe. Billions of years ago, every planet, star, and human being was just a bunch of atoms bound tightly together somewhere in the center of the universe. That infinitely dense speck blew up and spread across space, eventually forming everything in the world and beyond. So technically, you are a star, even if you'll never be famous.

REASON: The Big Bang is the penis responsible for a remarkable sexual experience in a woman's life. This event could be the first "bang" that started it all, or it could be a singular sexual experience that really blows her top. Either way, this name belongs to the dick responsible for the most memorable lay in a person's life. The Big Bang is something special that a woman will never forget.

RATING: 🍆

BIG DIPPER

ORIGIN: What we in the Northern Hemisphere call the Big Dipper is a constellation that is recognized by many cultures across the globe as being a significant symbol and a practical guide for travelers. It's also one of the easiest constellations to spot in the sky, so impress your date by pointing it out, then make your move.

REASON: The stars that form the Big Dipper are alternately known as the Bear or the Plow in certain places. Have a sky-high good time as the Big Dipper dips, buries, and plows his way into that special someone.

RATING: 🍆

BINARY STAR

ORIGIN: A binary star system consists of a pair of stars that orbit a shared point in space. The brighter star is called the primary, and the other is its companion star. Binary stars are popular in science fiction movies like *Star Wars* because they make everything seem more space-tastic.

REASON: The Binary Star is affected by the gravitational pull of both girls and guys. He rises up when his partner brings a companion to share the bed. Depending on your sex and which way you swing, if you're with a Binary Star there's a good chance you'll be sleeping with several celestial bodies.

RATING:

HORSEHEAD NEBULA

ORIGIN: A nebula is a giant cloud of dust that blocks out background light. The Horsehead Nebula is located in the constellation Orion, and as its name indicates, it resembles the head of a horse.

REASON: A Horsehead Nebula is a penis that you might mistake for a horse's cock. It's wild and has a reputation for bucking anyone who tries to ride it, but that just makes taming one a worthwhile achievement.

RATING:

JUPITER

ORIGIN: Jupiter is the largest planet in the solar system. It's about eleven times the size of Earth, though it's not as dense. It is a gas giant, meaning that, though it has a rocky core, the majority of the planet is made up of hydrogen, which would be deadly for a human to breathe. The planet is named after the Roman king of the gods.

REASON: A guy with a Jupiter has a big dick, but he's also a fat-ass with a gas problem. He has a nasty habit of thinking it's acceptable to fart around women who made the mistake of letting him sleep with them. Ladies, deflate this gassy giant's ego—and his "Jupiter"—by kicking him outside and changing the locks.

RATING: 🌀

LEO

ORIGIN: In astrology, Leo is the sign of the lion and a symbol of masculinity. The constellation of Leo was imagined as the figure of a lion by cultures as diverse as the Greeks, Egyptians, and Sumerians. The only other Leo who has come close to this level of fame is our modern-day superstar, Leonardo DiCaprio.

REASON: A man with a Leo is the King of the Jungle as well as the bedroom. His favorite type of feline lets him roar and roam across the sheets like they're the plains of Africa, and then lets him fall asleep on a sunny spot on the carpet. Just be aware that a Leo isn't a one-cat kind of dick; he has a pride of pussy at all times.

RATING: 🔨

MOON

ORIGIN: The Moon is Earth's only natural satellite, and is notable for being the largest satellite in our solar system relative to the size of its planet. Its prominence in the sky has always held a fascination for humans, who long ago realized its relationship to Earth's tides and seasons.

REASON: The Moon is a dick that is looking for ass-play. He likes his lovers to keep their moon base clean—and reciprocate in kind. But if he expects a woman to say "The eagle has landed!" every time he enters her rear end, she shouldn't feel bad exiting the Moon's orbit.

RATING:

SCORPIO

ORIGIN: The sign of Scorpio—the cosmic scorpion—signifies an abundance of passion and determination. The flip side of this sign is stubbornness. Passionate people's emotions run hot and cold, so you never know what you're going to get with a Scorpio.

REASON: A Scorpio is likely to shower a woman with affection, but this penis is just as likely to sting with his tail. But if getting stung in the backside is your style, then turn around and prepare to get pierced.

RATING:

SUPERNOVA

ORIGIN: A supernova is the release of light and energy after a star explodes; it is one of the most powerful events in the universe. Now if only the band Oasis would explain what the lyrics to "Champagne Supernova" mean, the universe could find balance.

REASON: A Supernova is a penis that causes an explosion of epic proportions. Ladies, if your partner's penis blinds you, then makes you see stars, you've found the right nickname.

RATING:

WHITE DWARF

ORIGIN: A white dwarf is a small star that is nearing the end of its evolutionary cycle. They are tiny relative to other stars, but they are also extremely dense, hot, and bright.

REASON: A White Dwarf is a short penis that is very thick and hard. He makes up for his lack of length with desperate enthusiasm, as though every sexual act could be his last.

RATING:

Comics & Cartoon Names

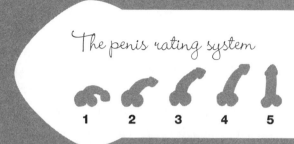

The penis rating system

1 2 3 4 5

If you don't take sex too seriously and like to laugh it up with your partner, choosing a name from the world of comics and cartoons might be right for you. What better way to show how much you care for that penis in your life than by giving him a name inspired by a favorite Saturday-morning cartoon show? If your idea of a perfect weekend is staying in bed all morning, watching cartoons, and playing with a really fun toy, then this is the chapter for you.

BUGS BUNNY

ORIGIN: Bugs Bunny is the beloved wascally rabbit of Looney Tunes fame. Bugs is a classic troublemaker who has influenced future class clowns from Ferris Bueller to Bart Simpson.

REASON: Bugs Bunny is the class clown who always gets away with his shenanigans. Ladies, he's not too shy to show you what's up, Doc. He also loves to dig into your holes with his thick carrot.

RATING:

CAPTAIN CAVEMAN

ORIGIN: Captain Caveman was a Hannah-Barbara cartoon covered in hair who saved the day along with his three female companions. There is probably more than one girl out there who looked up to this flying caveman superhero who ruled over Saturday-morning cartoons in the eighties.

REASON: A real-life Captain Caveman is rough around the edges but perfect for the girl who likes some loving of (pre)historic proportions.

RATING:

CARE BEAR

ORIGIN: Each cute and cuddly Care Bear has a unique color and a symbol on its tummy that represents its personality. Care Bears were created in 1981 for a line of greeting cards, but their success led to a massive merchandising empire of plush toys, an animated series that ran from 1985 to 1988, and three feature films. Even rival eighties icons My Little Pony couldn't withstand the sickeningly sweet power of the Care Bear Stare.

REASON: The man with a Care Bear is adorable, but he's still just a cub. He may be too soft to get the job done right. He's a good guy for a girl to have around when she's in need of some tenderness to cheer her up, but she should keep looking if what she needs is some rough lovin' from a grown bear.

RATING:

CHILLY WILLY

ORIGIN: Chilly Willy is an adorable little cartoon penguin living in snowy Alaska who loves pancakes. Those frosty arctic temperatures must be too cold even for a penguin, which explains why Chilly Willy is always portrayed sporting a knit hat and mittens on his flippers.

REASON: Cold temperatures cause chilly little willies to shrivel up into their bodies and disappear. Willy suffers from shrinkage, so do him a favor and turn the thermostat up.

RATING:

ELMER FUDD

ORIGIN: Looney Tunes's Elmer Fudd is a dimwitted hunter who is always on the prowl for Bugs Bunny. Old Elmer made it impossible for bald guys with lisps to get laid for years.

REASON: A man with an Elmer Fudd is pretty pathetic: He's been the butt of hundreds of pranks and it seems that his gun always misfires. An Elmer Fudd has trouble finding—and getting into—a lady's special spot no matter how hard he hunts for it.

RATING:

FOGHORN LEGHORN

ORIGIN: Foghorn Leghorn is the Looney Tunes's oversized rooster with a Southern drawl who was infamous for his pranks against the barnyard dog and for scoring with all the hens in the chicken house. He is a cartoon cross between Colonel Sanders and Bill Clinton.

REASON: A man with a Foghorn is a good old boy with a smooth voice, gentlemanly manners, and a third leg so sophisticated that women will want to blow it like a horn. Go ahead, ladies, it's the polite thing to do.

RATING:

FRED FLINTSTONE

ORIGIN: Fred Flintstone is the cartoon world's leading man of the prehistoric animated sitcom, *The Flintstones*. He is loud, brash, and sometimes loutish, but he's always a lovable family man.

REASON: A Fred Flintsone is like a rock in a guy's pocket. Some lucky lady will yell "yabba dabba doo!" when she finds out they didn't call it the "Stone Age" for nothing.

RATING:

GOOFY

ORIGIN: Goofy is a classic Walt Disney character introduced in 1932 in the short movie *Mickey's Revue*. Goofy and his pals Mickey Mouse and Donald Duck make up what may be the greatest trio in the world of cartoons. Goofy continues to entertain new generations of kids with his antics.

REASON: A guy with a Goofy penis is a klutz, but that can be lovable. It may take a few times for a Goofy to figure out where it needs to go, but if a woman plays with this guy's Goof-balls he'll be well on his way.

RATING:

THE GRAPE APE

ORIGIN: The Grape Ape is a gigantic purple gorilla Hanna-Barbera cartoon from the seventies. *Grape Ape* was part of a wonderful tradition of that era when stoned cartoonists animated their weed-inspired daydreams for impressionable young children.

REASON: A dick that becomes big and turns a shade of purple when turned-on deserves this name. Soak this penis in grape flavoring or wrap it in a purple condom for a real treat.

RATING:

GUMBY

ORIGIN: Gumby is a little figure made of green clay that, despite being a little creepy, has become an icon of popular culture since his creation over fifty years ago. He has been featured in television, movies, and video games, but his first appearance was on *The Howdy Doody Show*. The Gumby shorts were a hit, and soon after he got his own series, *The Adventures of Gumby*, which was the first TV show to use clay animation. Gumby's whimsical and adventurous personality is based on the Gingerbread Man, but he's not edible, so keep an eye on the clay-eating kids.

REASON: A Gumby penis is a green, diseased dick. Women should wash their hands if he gets any of his gross gummy goo on them. This blockhead needs a prescription for penicillin, but no one should wait around for him to cure his sick dick.

RATING: 🍆

INSPECTOR GADGET

ORIGIN: Inspector Gadget was a clumsy detective outfitted with a seemingly endless array of bionic gadgets that was the star of a TV cartoon series. He wasn't capable of solving his cases with real detective work, but his gadgets—and his niece Penny—always saved the day.

REASON: A guy with an Inspector Gadget doesn't know everything he's doing in the bedroom, but he knows enough to come with a backup plan. Go-go gadget vibrator!

RATING: 🍆

MARVIN THE MARTIAN

ORIGIN: Marvin is an extraterrestrial from Mars who is hell-bent on destroying Earth. Despite appearing in just a handful of the original Looney Tunes cartoons, he's developed a devoted following, as can be seen by the abundance of his airbrushed likenesses on oversized T-shirts at theme parks.

REASON: There are some nights out when a beautiful woman just has to beat the hotties back with a stick. Then there are other nights when she ends up with the biggest creep in the room trying out his magic tricks in an attempt to show her his uncircumcised, helmet-wearing Marvin the Martian. Ladies, do not let this alien inside your spaceship.

RATING: 🍆

MR. BURNS

ORIGIN: *The Simpsons*'s Mr. Burns is the incredibly wealthy and devious elder of Springfield. Mr. Burns's moral compass is always pointing south, whether he's trying to block out the sun or destroy the moon for his own profit.

REASON: A guy with a Mr. Burns is either a cranky old man or a young dude with wrinkly, ugly balls and a stick up his ass. Erase this cock from your life ASAP.

RATING: 🍆

ODIE

ORIGIN: Odie is the good-natured but dimwitted dog that is a regular character in the *Garfield* comic strip. Odie's trademarks are a huge slobbering tongue lolling out of his mouth and an always-present grin. He seems to be the only animal in the *Garfield* world unable to talk,

but he has been known to have rare flashes of brilliance, which usually appear to foil one of Garfield's schemes.

REASON: A cock named Odie belongs to a guy who is cute and sweet, but also as dumb as a dog with a lobotomy. He's loyal so he'll treat you right and the sex can be amazing, but don't expect any stimulating pillow talk. In addition, an Odie always comes when called—how's that for obedience?

RATING: 🍆

OPTIMUS PRIME

ORIGIN: Optimus Prime is the leader of the good Transformers, a line of toys that change back and forth from a robot into some type of vehicle. The Transformers later starred in a TV cartoon series of the same name.

REASON: Transformers are great because they are two toys in one. A penis named Optimus Prime may start off the night acting like a good boy, but by the time he's finished he's been transformed into a sex machine.

RATING:

PAPA SMURF

ORIGIN: Papa Smurf is the tiny, bearded leader of the diminutive blue Smurfs. The Belgian cartoonist Peyo created the Smurfs in 1953.

REASON: Papa Smurf is old and wise, but that doesn't mean he's slow. In fact, Papa Smurf is quite spry for his age. If you have an older gentleman caller with a proud white beard of pubes surrounding his Smurf, then say hello to Papa.

RATING:

POPEYE

ORIGIN: The world's most famous cartoon sailorman, Popeye slurps down cans of spinach to become ridiculously strong so he can beat down his nemesis Bluto.

REASON: Women are like spinach to a Popeye dick, because eating them makes it get big and strong. Ladies, if you're looking for a man with a Popeye, be on the lookout for big forearms, because big forearms mean a big penis.

RATING:

PORKY PIG

ORIGIN: Porky Pig was created in 1935 for Looney Tunes and quickly became a star of the animated world. He gave the often-maligned pig a famous mascot and probably saved a few swine hides.

REASON: Guys aren't the only chubby chasers out there. Girls like a hunk with some chunk too. A penis named Porky Pig is fat and pink, and he'll make any woman squeal.

RATING:

SCOOBY

ORIGIN: Scooby-Doo is the cartoon dog superstar of one of the longest-running franchises in Hanna-Barbera's history. The Great Dane with a speech impediment made his first appearance in the original series, *Scooby-Doo, Where Are You?* in 1969. Scooby is a loyal and good dog, but he spends a lot of time acting like a scaredy-cat.

REASON: A penis named Scooby may seem shy at first, but once he trusts a woman, she won't find him in someone else's bed. Every orgasm a Scooby gives is like another Scooby snack to enjoy.

RATING:

SHAGGY

ORIGIN: Shaggy is the slacker member of the Scooby-Doo gang, and comedic foil to goody two-shoes Fred. Hero of stoners everywhere? Yes. Heroic? No. Shaggy is probably as well known for being the coward who ran at the first sign of evil theme-park owners in disguise as ghosts as he is for loving Scooby snacks.

REASON: Shaggy is a lazy penis who is too tired to keep himself neat and clean. His base is full of unkempt hair that looks like a set of dreadlocks from a Phish show. Zoinks!

RATING:

SPEEDY GONZALES

ORIGIN: Speedy Gonzales is a mucho rapido mouse that appeared in his first Looney Tunes cartoon in 1953. He was usually seen outwitting Sylvester the cat while propagating politically incorrect Mexican stereotypes.

REASON: A man with a Speedy is fast—in fact, he's too fast in the sack. Not only that, but he's also as small as a mouse. He's not even worth a quick romp in the hay, because he's so tiny you'll never know he was there!

RATING: 🐾

SPONGEBOB SQUAREPANTS

ORIGIN: SpongeBob is the nicest and most innocent toon that lives under the sea. He lives in a pineapple too, which is a cool choice of accommodations when you live on the ocean floor.

REASON: A square with a SpongeBob SquarePants is a sexually inexperienced nerd who has trouble finding his way around a woman's body of water. He's nice and all, but his childlike ways have no place in the dirty adult world we live in.

RATING: 🐾

THE TASMANIAN DEVIL

ORIGIN: This Looney Tunes character is an unintelligible wild animal that crashes through walls, trees, and everything else standing in his way.

REASON: A man with a Tasmanian Devil will be familiar to anyone who has dated a frat guy. His dick is a maniac that loves to party, and once a woman gets this wild man spinning like a top he'll be all over her through the night.

RATING:

WALDO

ORIGIN: The Waldo books are childhood classics that feature Waldo, a world traveler. Waldo's picture is hidden somewhere among fantastically illustrated scenes from all over the globe. The goal of the books is to find Waldo among the dense drawings.

REASON: If the guy a woman is with takes off his red-and-white-striped pants and all she can think is "Where's Waldo?" then she needs to send this traveler back to the street.

RATING:

WILE E. COYOTE

ORIGIN: This Looney Tunes coyote's destiny is to chase the Roadrunner, but never catch him. It would be tragic if it weren't so damn entertaining.

REASON: A guy who chases after an unfortunate woman and gets past all her best defenses until he's finally got her captured in his trap has a dick named Wile E. Coyote. Being chased by this penis is half the fun. The other half is when this penis is accompanied by a bag of Acme tricks and contraptions to use during sex.

RATING:

WOODY WOODPECKER

ORIGIN: Woody Woodpecker is a screwball cartoon character that premiered in animated shorts in 1940. The earliest version of Woody

Woodpecker was a completely insane, roughly drawn bird that annoyed the hell out of everyone he met. He evolved into a more refined-looking bird whose personality was smoothed over; this version of Woody used his jackhammer beak on deserving antagonists.

REASON: This name pretty much says it all. The cartoon Woody is a screwy bird, but the pecker deserving this name is as hard as wood and has the stamina to pound away at any woman's hole.

RATING:

Historical Names

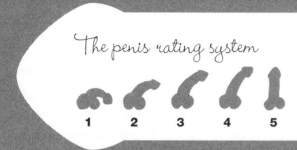

The penis rating system

1 2 3 4 5

A lot of people look back on historical figures through rose-colored glasses and assume that just because they appear in a black-and-white photograph that they must have been prudes. But it's important to note that even four score and seven years ago our forefathers were probably trying to put their foreskin in everything that moved. A name from yesteryear will give a penis the appearance of credibility while disguising its perverted mind.

AL CAPONE

ORIGIN: Brooklyn's original notorious gangster blasted his way across the United States to take control of the Chicago mob in the 1920s. Al Capone broke every law of Prohibition until he was arrested and brought to justice by Elliot Ness. Ironically, income tax evasion was the charge that finally put Capone behind bars.

REASON: Anyone sucking on an Al Capone should be careful, because his funky spunk is as nasty as a batch of bad bootleg liquor. Don't say we didn't warn you if your next blowjob causes you to go blind.

RATING:

BUSH

ORIGIN: The first decade of the twenty-first century was one of the most trying times in American history. The country needed a strong and wise leader that could unite a nation and shepherd it through the difficult time. Instead we got President George W. Bush. Though the country's infrastructure decayed and banks collapsed, the one bright area was comedy. It was a boom time for late-night joke writers and Bush impressionists.

REASON: A Bush isn't the sharpest tool in the shed, but when he gets an idea in his head he can't be dissuaded. If he sets his sights on a woman, she needs to make sure he wears a condom; he typically just plows ahead into his lover without thinking of the consequences until she kicks him out of her bed.

RATING:

CAESAR

ORIGIN: Julius Caesar seized absolute control of Rome, ending its longstanding democratic rule and becoming its first emperor in centuries. He was beloved by the majority of Rome's citizens; however, his enemies in the Senate called him a tyrant, and he was murdered by a group of senators that included Brutus, whom he had trusted as a friend. Brutus gave us the English word *brute* and Caesar gave us a beloved salad, so it's clear whose legacy came out on top.

REASON: People may think that Caesar is a tyrannical jerk, but a cock named Caesar is the ruler of the known world because he loves to toss a lady's salad. All hail Caesar!

RATING:

COLUMBUS

ORIGIN: In 1492 Christopher Columbus sailed the ocean blue to discover the New World and give Americans a day off from work and school every October.

REASON: Today, a Columbus is a cock that sails around the freshman dorm looking for innocent girls to screw. He likes to have sex with virgins just so he can say he was the first one there. Unless you want this dick to plant his flag in you, send him back to the old world.

RATING:

EINSTEIN

ORIGIN: Albert Einstein had the biggest brain in history. His theories of relativity have been confusing would-be physicists for over a century.

REASON: We all know what a big brain means, right? Well it has nothing to do with dick size, but this intelligent cock can figure out what he needs to do to keep a woman satisfied. And if an Einstein happens to be a smaller than average penis, he's smart enough to step aside for the perfect vibrator to keep a woman more than happy.

RATING:

FREUD

ORIGIN: Freud is the father of modern psychiatry. He popularized "talk" therapy and emphasized the influence of one's early experiences on the psyche. Freud is the reason therapists want to know about their patients' mothers, and he's also the reason why people think last night's dream is so important.

REASON: Freud is the dick you can thank for making you think you're crazy. A Freud is so good at what he does that he can cause a host of mental problems like obsession and sex-mania. Women have also been known to suffer from depression when he's not around.

RATING:

GANDHI

ORIGIN: Gandhi led India to independence from the British via peaceful means. India was the jewel in the crown of the British Empire, but Gandhi's love-based leadership forced the Brits to give it up. He was a hippie before it was trendy.

REASON: Gandhi was a lover, not a fighter. He's also the patron saint of sexy bald guys. In fact, women are lining up to rub his head. Ladies, if you succumb to him without protest, this dick will have a sit-in on your face.

RATING:

GEORGE WASHINGTON

ORIGIN: George Washington was a founding father, America's most famous war hero and first president, and an all around great guy. According to a famous—but probably untrue—legend, he chopped down a cherry tree as a boy and when confronted, didn't lie about what he'd done.

REASON: The penis that is given the name of the great George Washington happens to have a reputation for taking down more than one virgin's cherry. He's attached to an upstanding guy, but certainly not an angel. He'll be your founding father if you call him daddy.

RATING:

HENRY VIII

ORIGIN: Henry VIII is known as a brutal king of England for beheading two of his wives, killing off his enemies in droves, and being excommunicated from the Catholic Church for establishing the Church of England so he could get a divorce.

REASON: A man with a Henry rules the bedroom with an iron fist, which can be fun for his partner once or twice if she's into the rough stuff, but

ultimately his selfish ways will drive her away. His mighty dick has the heft of a swinging ax, but, ladies, if he starts calling you "Anne Boleyn," protect your neck and find a new guy.

RATING:

JACKSON POLLOCK

ORIGIN: Jackson Pollock became one of the twentieth century's most famous painters with the iconoclastic art he created by dripping and splattering paint on a canvas laid out flat on the floor. His haters kicked off the "I could do that" critique movement.

REASON: A Jackson Pollock in the boudoir creates artwork out of the mess he makes on his lover. Ladies, that splatter he left on your belly could be worth something someday, so have him sign it with his big paintbrush.

RATING:

JFK

ORIGIN: A cult of personality surrounds President John F. Kennedy that grows larger with every successive year since his death. His presidency was so admired and idolized that it was dubbed Camelot in his time. JFK was also a notorious ladies' man who famously bedded Marilyn Monroe.

REASON: JFK is a high-society dick that likes to f**k. He's a rich, handsome, and charming penis. Ladies, hum "Happy Birthday, Mr. President" to this cock and you'll be the one who gets a big gift.

RATING:

LBJ

ORIGIN: Lyndon Baines Johnson succeeded JFK to the presidency in 1963. He oversaw turbulent times in the White House, including the escalation of the Vietnam War, the passing of civil rights laws, and progressive changes to the fabric of American government. He used coercion and tough-guy tactics to get his agenda passed.

REASON: This dick loves blow-jobs. Fast, slow, wet or dry, an LBJ doesn't care how, he just wants to put himself in a mouth. This dick travels the world looking to get himself sucked. He has a reputation south of the border, where he's known as El BJ, presidente de sexo.

RATING:

MARCO POLO

ORIGIN: The Italian Marco Polo opened Europe to Far East trade in the thirteenth century. He traveled across distant lands and discovered an exciting world rarely seen by outsiders. However, he is now mainly remembered by the backyard pool game that took his name. Marco!

REASON: Marco is a dick who enjoys a lot of bush, mainly because he loves going down and searching east and west for hidden places. There's no need to shave all your hair off when you have Marco Polo exploring your body.

RATING:

NEIL ARMSTRONG

ORIGIN: Neil Armstrong became internationally famous and a modern American hero for being the first person to walk on the moon. Other men have accomplished this feat since then, but we'll always remember Neil Armstrong's name above all for being the first.

REASON: Neil Armstrong is an appropriate name for the penis that a woman loses her anal virginity to. After all ladies, this is the first dick to plant his flag. Give this cock extra points by dramatically declaring,

"Houston, the eagle has landed" (on your moon), once the deed is done.

RATING:

PABLO PICASSO

ORIGIN: Pablo Picasso is the most famous artist of modern times for his revolutionary style of painting. He was also infamously known for his volatile relationships with the many women in his life.

REASON: We can't promise a woman that the video she makes starring her and the Pablo Picasso penis will be worth millions someday, but we can guarantee that she'll have an occasionally stormy relationship. The Picasso will drive her mad sometimes, but the two will also make beautiful and sexy art together.

RATING:

SLICK WILLY

ORIGIN: Bill Clinton has a reputation for having a silver tongue. He mastered the art of telling people what they want to hear and he also has an uncanny ability to escape from serious political harm, both of which gave him the nickname Slick Willy. Even though Clinton hasn't been in office since 1999, his sexual antics with a certain twenty-two-year-old intern granted him permanent status as one of Jay Leno's favorite punch lines. Clinton may have treated the White House like his own personal spring break, but perhaps it's his fallibility that is so relatable and makes up the cornerstone of his charm.

REASON: A Slick Willy will slip himself inside an intern and make a mess of her dress before she can say "Thank you, Mr. President." The affair will probably be dirty and inappropriate, but on the plus side he'll take the lucky lady out for a Big Mac after having sex.

RATING:

TEDDY

ORIGIN: Theodore ("Teddy") Roosevelt has one of the most colorful images among American presidents. Frequently bedridden with asthma as a boy, Teddy spent his life focused on self-improvement, adventure, and study. He was a soldier, a cowboy, a historian, and a trust-busting president, but perhaps his most lasting legacy is the "teddy bear," a term coined after Roosevelt showed compassion for a black bear during a hunt.

REASON: Roosevelt was famous for his saying "speak softly and carry a big stick," so Teddy is the right name for a penis that lets his big stick do all the talking. A man with a Teddy is a cowboy who is perfectly happy in the outdoors and likes to have sex out on the range, but he's also a soft bear of a guy who is perfect for snuggling.

RATING:

TRICKY DICK

ORIGIN: Richard Nixon had one of the longest-running political careers in American history and as the thirty-seventh president of the United States achieved improved relations with China and the Soviet Union. Unfortunately, no one remembers that about Tricky Dick Nixon. His legacy is the Watergate scandal, in which he condoned a break-in at the headquarters of the Democratic Party. Nixon was implicated in a cover-up of the shenanigans and as a result resigned from the presidency.

REASON: You can't trust a Tricky Dick. He'll lie and cheat to break into a girl's pants and when he does—surprise!—she'll find out he's been secretly taping her during sex and posting it online. Ladies, impeach this cock and find another dick to deep throat.

RATING:

WAVY GRAVY

ORIGIN: Wavy Gravy will always be a hippie icon for being the MC at Woodstock and for being a part of the Grateful Dead's entourage. His baby boomer cred got even higher when a Ben & Jerry's ice cream flavor was named after him.

REASON: A guy with a Wavy Gravy dick likes girls who are all natural in every way. He loves a girl in her birthday suit with a "Hair"-y bush. This guy will treat his woman like his flower child. He'll turn her on and take her on a sexual hallucination-filled ride on his Wavy Gravy train.

RATING:

WILD BILL HICKOK

ORIGIN: Wild Bill was famous in the Old West for being a lawman, gunslinger, and gambler. He was a real man of his times, who was famous for having duels at noon. His rough and tumble life eventually caught up with him when he was killed during a poker game.

REASON: These days a Wild Bill is a crazy penis that loves having day sex at high noon and is a sharp-shooter in the bedroom. Have fun with this dick, but don't bet on him providing a stable relationship.

RATING:

THE WRIGHT BROTHERS

ORIGIN: Brothers Orville and Wilbur Wright invented the first working airplane. Their flight on December 17, 1903, in Kitty Hawk, North Carolina, was the first powered, controlled, and sustained flight of human beings in history. Without these two there would be no Mile High Club.

REASON: Ladies, if being with two dicks sounds good to you, then climb aboard with this duo. Being with the Wright brothers means you're in the middle of a sibling double team. Go ahead, be part of a Wright Brothers sandwich.

RATING:

Musical Names

The penis rating system

1 2 3 4 5

Musicians are renowned for their sexual exploits and appetites. The penis names in this chapter tap into that sexual mojo and help serenade you into a wild night of passion. These names will make some lucky lady want to wield an ax, blow a horn, and bang a drum. Cock Stars only need audition for these names.

AXL (ROSE)

ORIGIN: Axl had a short-lived but stunning run as one of the biggest rock stars of all time until his band Guns N' Roses broke up. After that, he pretty much went into hibernation, only to appear about as frequently as a groundhog. Axl had passionate but volatile relationships with his model girlfriends and the paparazzi, who took their lives into their own hands with every attempt at a photograph.

REASON: A woman will be the sweet child for Axl if she chooses to be with this bed-rocking dick. It will be a brief but fiery relationship that will feel like Paradise City one day, and will have her screaming "welcome to the jungle!" the next. One thing's for sure though: With an Axl, she'll never have to ask, "Where do we go?"

RATING:

THE BOSS

ORIGIN: In New Jersey, the Boss isn't the head of the mob, he is Bruce Springsteen. The Boss began in little Asbury Park, New Jersey, but his songs, like "Born in the USA" and "Thunder Road," turned him into an American rock icon famous throughout the world. A Springsteen concert is epic, lasting for hours on end, turning his shows into all-night parties.

REASON: All-American, passionate, and sexy, the Boss is fully in charge in the bedroom. The Boss's stamina is epic and women will have fun working for this dick all night long.

RATING:

BUFFALO SOLDIER

ORIGIN: Buffalo Soldier was the nickname for the U.S. Army's black cavalry during the Indian Wars of the late 1800s. Bob Marley's song of the same name honored these soldiers. Marley identified with the Buffalo Soldiers' struggle to succeed in the world as a minority.

REASON: The Buffalo Soldier is a penis as big as a buffalo that rides its lover like a horse.

RATING:

ELVIS

ORIGIN: Music was never the same after Elvis Presley shook his hips. Teenagers' loins awakened, and parents were up in arms. Elvis represents the scary and revolutionary freedom of being a teenager through his music.

REASON: A guy with an Elvis is a Southern fried rockabilly lover, a hound dog, and a horn-dog. Women should get with this dick in his youthful days while he's still rocking his hips, or they'll end up with an overweight Vegas lounge act in a sequined jumpsuit—er, condom.

RATING:

JOHNNY B. GOODE

ORIGIN: "Johnny B. Goode" by Chuck Berry is considered one of the greatest songs of all time and has influenced pretty much everyone who's picked up a guitar. It's been covered widely by a range of musicians, from Elvis to Marty McFly in *Back to the Future*.

REASON: One of the most covered songs in rock and roll, "Johnny B. Goode" tells the story of a country boy who could wail on the guitar. A guy who has a woman singing his praises in the bedroom has a penis worthy of this moniker. Go Johnny, go go go!

RATING: 1

JOHNNY ROTTEN

ORIGIN: Johnny Rotten is the legendary frontman of the punk-rocking Sex Pistols. He terrorized both the establishment and personal cleanliness. The out-of-tune singer earned his nickname from his lack of oral hygiene, proving an unfortunate British stereotype true.

REASON: Johnny Rotten is a disgusting, dirty dick. Send him to the doctor to get a shot of penicillin.

RATING:

LA BAMBA

ORIGIN: "La Bamba" is a Mexican folk song that became one of rock 'n' roll's best-known tunes when it was covered by Ritchie Valens. The song had a revival in 1987 when Valens's life story was adapted into a movie starring Lou Diamond Phillips.

REASON: La Bamba roughly translated means "to shake," and that's just what a woman's body does when she's with this Latin penis. Be careful though, ladies: He'll drop a love bomb on you.

RATING:

LED ZEPPELIN

ORIGIN: Classic rock's most hardpartying band trashed more hotels than Jim Morrison and scored with more groupies than the Rolling Stones. Led Zeppelin is the rock god standard by which every subsequent band is judged.

REASON: A Led Zeppelin dick is rock 'n' roll. The sex is loud and trashy, but this penis makes a woman feel like she's on a stairway to heaven all night long.

RATING:

LITTLE RICHARD

ORIGIN: Little Richard is one of the godfathers of rock 'n' roll. He may be most known for being short and flamboyant, but his music ("Tutti Frutti," "Good Golly Miss Molly") should never be forgotten for laying the foundation for modern music by adding funk to a rock beat.

REASON: Short and effeminate can work for a rock idol, but they are not good qualities for a penis. This tutti-frutti dick is probably not a good choice as a woman's lover, but he could make a fabulous best friend.

RATING:

MEATLOAF

ORIGIN: Meatloaf wrote epic songs of love and passion. He is also the least likely rock star, as far as looks go, due to his girth.

REASON: A woman sleeping with this dick has probably experienced paradise by the dashboard lights. A Meatloaf is great for sex in a car; he may not look that hot, but he's large enough to make even the most awkward position magic. A man with a Meatloaf may love a lady in the backseat, but will he love her forever? It's safe to say, "No, he won't do that."

RATING:

METHOD MAN

ORIGIN: Method Man is the most well known member of the Wu-Tang Clan, Staten Island's premiere hip-hop collective. He took the charisma he displays in his music and has evolved into an actor on TV and film, creating a brand for himself that is anything but by the book.

REASON: The real Meth is super-cool, but a Method Man in the bed is smoked out, boring, and conventional. This dick needs to sober up and be a little less by the book (enough with the rhythm method already!) if he wants to be a star.

RATING: 🖕

MOTORHEAD

ORIGIN: The English heavy metal group Motorhead emerged in the late seventies and, along with their pal Ozzy Osbourne, quickly established themselves as leaders of the English hard-rock scene. They're one of the longest-lasting rock bands as well, having formed in 1975 and continuing to this day with hits like "Ace of Spades."

REASON: A Motorhead is a dick that rocks and rolls like an engine. He's an all-natural vibrator, so you never have to worry about running out of batteries.

RATING: 🖕

NIRVANA

ORIGIN: Buddhists describe Nirvana as a perfect state of mind, but the name was co-opted by one of the most successful and influential bands of the nineties. Nirvana never seemed comfortable with their enormous success and label as the voice of Generation X. The group came to a sad end with the suicide of singer Kurt Cobain.

REASON: Women don't have to be with a sullen, grungy guy in order to reach Nirvana; they just need someone to let them come as they are. Sleeping with a guy with a Nirvana is good karma and will help reincarnate you as a sexual guru.

RATING:

OZZY

ORIGIN: Ozzy Osbourne wasn't always a doddering, mumbling father in an MTV docu-sitcom. There was a time when Ozzy was the Prince of Darkness of the music industry who ate the heads off chickens onstage and terrified parents into thinking their children were listening to satanic music.

REASON: A dude with an Ozzy is scary-sexy. Ladies, feel free to jump on board this crazy train and get freaky like a devil from Oz.

RATING:

PINK FLOYD

ORIGIN: The members of Pink Floyd were the mad priests of classic rock. Their style of psychedelic blues-rock is a natural high that doesn't require a drug enhancement to feel like a trip — but partaking in some sort of illicit substance is recommended before you listen to *Dark Side of the Moon* while watching *The Wizard of Oz*.

REASON: Perhaps it's because this cock looks just like a magic mushroom, but getting with a penis named Pink Floyd feels like falling into a trippy sexual hallucination.

RATING:

PRINCE

ORIGIN: Rock star Prince looks like he's only four feet tall, but he's got a giant amount of sexually explicit material in that body. In the heyday of eighties rock, Prince and Madonna were the king and queen of sexually charged music and shocking displays of skin.

REASON: Prince is a very short, slightly androgynous dick with huge sex appeal. Despite his tiny stature, this dick has the confidence of a penis twice his size. Ladies, you can be his dirty Diana if

you don't mind getting wet from his purple rain.

RATING:

RICO SUAVE

ORIGIN: Ecuadorian rapper Gerardo was a one-hit wonder, but he left his mark on history with his song "Rico Suave," the spiciest dance track of the early nineties. Looking back now, the song seems embarrassingly cheesy, but in its heyday every guy wanted to be "Rich & Smooth."

REASON: Rico Suave is the alter ego for a Latin lover's spicy dick. By day he is an average Joe with an average life. But when the sun goes down this cock becomes a Don Juan in the bedroom.

RATING:

SGT. PECKER (AND HIS LONELY HEARTS CLUB BAND)

ORIGIN: For their eighth album, *Sgt. Pepper's Lonely Hearts Club Band*, the Beatles created psychedelic-inspired alter egos for themselves. The album is considered one of the greatest of all time and is a perennial favorite of teenagers looking to get high with a little help from their friends.

REASON: Sgt. Pecker is all about peace and love, but he is a drill sergeant in bed. He'll have you doing pushups on top of him all night long.

RATING:

SNOOP

ORIGIN: Snoop Dogg was a gangster in his youth but he grew into an ambassador of hip-hop throughout the world. He's also become so synonymous with weed that he gets a free smoking pass wherever he goes.

REASON: A dick with a Snoop is the man, and women love his doggy style. Ladies, grab hold of your thug's joint and take a puff, sip on his gin and juice, and bow down to the big dog. He likes to talk dirty in bed and ask, "What's my name?"

RATING:

WHITESNAKE

ORIGIN: Lift up your lighter and sing along in tribute to hard rock's finest balladeers. These rockers inspired girls to writhe sexily on their boyfriends' cars in lingerie, just like on MTV. It's safe to say that these guys got into the rock game for the purest reason: to get laid.

REASON: Whitesnake is a great name for the penis of a guy with big eighties hair and ripped acid-washed jeans. He can be found tailgating in the parking lot of the Monsters of Rock tour. After a few cans of beer post-show his mullet might look half decent. We won't make fun of you too much for doing him in his Camaro.

RATING:

Animal Names

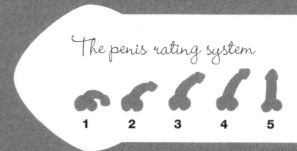

The penis rating system

1 2 3 4 5

Tap into your natural animal magnetism by choosing a name inspired by a furry friend. If you climb down the tree of evolution you'll find a rawer, more emotional state of being for your man's pants pet. Whether this dick is a beast of burden, or a teacher's pet, you'll find the right name for a wild man in this chapter.

BARRACUDA

ORIGIN: Barracudas are long, pike-like fish with a thick row of nasty, sharp teeth. These scavengers have a bad reputation for taking bites out of careless swimmers.

REASON: The Barracuda is a penis that can't get a woman excited enough to get her juices flowing. Being so dry means the Barracuda can leave a nasty bite before a woman fishes him out of her.

RATING:

BOA CONSTRICTOR

ORIGIN: The boa constrictor is a large snake most commonly found in the jungles of South America as well as in the bedrooms of weird, lonely men. Boas can grow up to thirteen feet in length and survive on rodents, birds, and lizards. They bite, strangle, and then swallow their victims whole, slowly digesting them over the course of several days.

REASON: The Boa Constrictor belongs to a guy who is way too attached to his woman. She'd leave this loser if his Boa Constrictor weren't so big that she could barely swallow it whole. So, okay, maybe she'll wait until tomorrow to break up with him.

RATING:

CURIOUS GEORGE

ORIGIN: Curious George is a character from a series of illustrated children's books about George, a monkey who lives with "the Man with the Yellow Hat" in the city. George is a mischievous monkey, so he's always getting into some type of high jinks, but the Man with the Yellow Hat always rescues him and brings him home safe and sound.

REASON: A Curious George penis is one that pops up and pokes around looking for trouble—usually in the morning when its love interest is trying to sleep off last night.

RATING:

DUMBO

ORIGIN: *Dumbo* is Walt Disney's classic animated film from 1941. The story is about a baby elephant born into a traveling circus whose ears are unusually large. The other elephants mock his large ears by nicknaming him "Dumbo," and his mother is put in a cage after defending her son. Things look pretty bleak until Dumbo accidentally gets drunk with his buddy Timothy the mouse one night and discovers that his gigantic ears allow him to fly. Dumbo's amazing feats of flight make him the star of the circus, and he lives happily ever after with Timothy and his mom.

REASON: A Dumbo dick is long and surrounded by large balls. If you see an elephant head when you look down at those cock and balls, then you've got a Dumbo on your hands.

RATING:

FLIPPER

ORIGIN: Flipper is the dolphin character of film (1963) and TV (1964–1967) stardom who we can confidently say is the most famous crime-fighting dolphin in the world. Flipper's legacy is evident today in the improved relationship between humans and dolphins.

REASON: Flipper the dolphin was adorable, but this name goes to a penis that is the opposite of adorable. A Flipper is a deformed dick, named for its resemblance to a dorsal fin. Disturbing, we know.

RATING:

MOBY DICK

ORIGIN: Moby Dick is literature's infamous white whale. Captain Ahab's obsession with the whale led to his death and that of his entire crew. A guy can only dream that his dick is so enticing that it would wreak that much havoc.

REASON: Moby Dick is an on-the-nose choice for a penis name, but a classic as good as this needs to be respected.

RATING: █

SEABISCUIT

ORIGIN: Seabiscuit was a champion racehorse recognized as one of the greatest horses in American racing as well as one of the most popular sports figures of his time. Seabiscuit and his jockey Red Pollard were both underdogs who overcame great odds in order to win, and Seabiscuit became a symbol of American strength.

REASON: A name like Seabiscuit is usually applied to a horse-sized cock. However, the name can also be used as an insult to describe a dick that comes to the finish line too fast.

RATING: TO █

SHAMU

ORIGIN: Shamu is the primary resident at Sea World and the most well known killer whale in the world. The first Shamu was brought to perform at San Diego's Sea World in 1965 and, after she died, her name was passed down to different killer whales at the park.

REASON: A Shamu is a lady-killer of a whale-sized dick. A woman is guaranteed to get wet if she's in his splash zone.

RATING: █

Food-Inspired Names

The penis rating system

1 2 3 4 5

Some penises are like sweet lollipops and others are sour lemonheads. Which one are you partial to? This chapter will help you name any type of penis, whether it is a quick guilty pleasure like a fast-food hamburger or an organically grown, nutritional granola bar.

BABY RUTH

ORIGIN: This candy bar concoction made with chocolate-covered peanuts, caramel, and nougat was first sold in 1921 by the Curtiss Candy Company. They claim that the candy bar was named after former President Grover Cleveland's daughter, Ruth, and not Babe Ruth the baseball player. However there is speculation that Curtiss made this claim in order not to have to pay royalties to the baseball player.

REASON: A Baby Ruth penis doesn't resemble a baseball bat at all. It looks more like a baby's finger. Yes, it might have some great nuts, but run the other way if a guy pulls this teeny weenie out of his pants.

RATING:

BAZOOKA JOE

ORIGIN: Bazooka Joe is a comic strip character and teenage cartoon mascot of Bazooka bubblegum. Bazooka Joe inexplicably wears an eye patch and appears in childish and humorless comics that accompany horrible-tasting gum.

REASON: Look at the similarities between the comic-strip character and a penis: they each have one eye, they come wrapped in a package, and you can put both of them in your mouth.

RATING:

THE BIG GULP

ORIGIN: The Big Gulp got its start in 1980 when 7-11 started offering soda in liter-sized cups. Additions to the Gulp family include the 44-ounce Super Big Gulp and the huge 2-liter Double Gulp. Though very popular in America, the Big Gulp flopped in Japan.

REASON: This name is unique in that it describes what happens to the recipient as opposed to the characteristics of the penis itself. A Big Gulp may be rare, but, ladies, if you stumble across a Super Big Gulp or a Double Gulp, be prepared.

RATING:

BIG MAC

ORIGIN: A McDonald's franchise owner in Pittsburgh created this signature sandwich to compete with the Bob's Big Boy burger. It was a huge hit and was subsequently put on menus across the country in 1967. Its ingredients were seared into America's collective memory by the jingle "Two all beef patties, special sauce, lettuce, cheese, pickles, onions on a sesame seed bun."

REASON: A Big Mac is an extra-large pimp of a penis. This order comes with extra special sauce.

RATING:

BOB'S BIG BOY

ORIGIN: Bob's Big Boy is a restaurant chain that was originally founded near Los Angeles in 1936 by Bob Wian. Its signature sandwich is the Big Boy, a double-decker cheeseburger, which appears on the menu at all of its restaurants. The chain's mascot—a chubby boy in checkered overalls holding a cheeseburger—was created in exchange for a free meal by a Warner Bros. Studios animator who was having lunch at the restaurant. Big Boy restaurants spread across the country and many are still in operation today.

REASON: This penis doesn't have to belong to a man named Bob to earn this name; he just needs to be a double-decker "Big Boy" that requires two hands to eat.

RATING:

BUTTERFINGER

ORIGIN: In 1923, the Curtiss Candy Company held a contest to choose the name for its new candy, a crunchy peanut-brittle-centered bar coated in chocolate. The name of the bar was the result of a contest held by the manufacturer. A customer, who was a bit of a klutz, suggested "butterfinger" and it stuck.

REASON: A Butterfinger is a klutz of a penis that slips right out of its lover, over and over again.

RATING:

DING DONG

ORIGIN: The Ding Dong is a hockey-puck-shaped chocolate cake with a cream filling that was introduced in 1934. The treat's name comes from the chiming bells that appeared in Hostess' first TV commercials.

REASON: A Ding Dong is a dick that is thicker than it is long. They are to be avoided at all costs— unless you have a hockey fetish.

RATING:

JAWBREAKER

ORIGIN: A type of round, hard candy made of many layers of different colors and flavors, Jawbreakers are too hard to bite, so they must be sucked or licked, thus the name. Jawbreaker is the American nickname for the gobstopper (*gob* is British slang for "mouth"), which has been around for over a century. The Everlasting Gobstopper is named after the candy in Roald Dahl's *Charlie and Chocolate Factory*.

REASON: Ladies, unless you want to visit the dentist, do not bite down on the Jawbreaker. He's too big for that, so just lick and suck gently for your own protection. You'll both appreciate it.

RATING:

LAFFY TAFFY

ORIGIN: First sold in the 1970s, Laffy Taffy was originally manufactured in thick square pieces. These days, the candy is shaped into long and thin rectangular pieces of taffy. Each piece has a cheesy joke written on the wrapper.

REASON: If some dude's soft, pliable dick gives you the chuckles, he has a Laffy Taffy.

RATING:

LUCKY CHARM

ORIGIN: After combining Cheerios with bits of Circus Peanuts, a General Mills employee hit upon the idea of a new cereal that had toasted oat pieces mixed with tiny marshmallow bits. Someone had the bright idea of shaping the marshmallows like the trinkets on a charm bracelet, and Lucky Charms was born.

REASON: You don't have to go to the end of the rainbow to find this penis, but you'll feel lucky to have it. It's magically delicious!

RATING:

MR. GOODBAR

ORIGIN: Hershey named their candy bar made of chocolate-coated peanuts the Mr. Goodbar. It inspired the title of *Looking for Mr. Goodbar*, a book adapted into an Oscar-nominated movie in 1977 starring Diane Keaton. No offense to Diane Keaton, but how could the producers not have cast Barbara Hershey? It seems like a lost opportunity.

REASON: The Mr. Goodbar penis is delicious and packed with nutty flavor. He's so good he deserves to be savored and enjoyed with long licks. Women shouldn't bite down on this sweet treat! If they're nice to him, he'll be very, very good to them in return.

RATING:

POWER BAR

ORIGIN: The PowerBar was the first energy bar on the market, and is now used by athletes the world over as part of their routine. An entrepreneur and his nutritionist girlfriend created it in their home kitchen. The bar was a big success, and the company was eventually bought by Nestlé.

REASON: The Power Bar penis shoots a big jolt of protein into its partner. It's a perfect quickie snack before a workout.

RATING:

PUDDING POP

ORIGIN: The frozen chocolaty confection the Pudding Pop will always be associated with its long-time spokesperson Bill Cosby, who introduced the treat to American kiddies in the 1980s. The pop was taken off the market during the 1990s but was then brought back due to popular demand. Long live the pop!

REASON: A Pudding Pop is a sweet-tasting, chocolate-colored penis pop. It is the perfect refreshment for a hot summer's day.

RATING:

RED BULL

ORIGIN: Red Bull is the most popular energy drink in the world. Based on a Thai drink, Red Bull is especially beloved by teenagers and computer nerds. In 2009, coca (the decocainized extract of a coca leaf) was found in Red Bull Cola produced in Germany. Red Bull admitted that their drink was made with "all natural" ingredients such as the unprocessed coca leaf. That Red Bull buzz is a real high!

REASON: Red Bull is a great name for a penis that's big, ruddy, and full of juice that comes complete with an energy buzz.

RATING:

TWINKIE

ORIGIN: Since 1930, Twinkies have been one of America's bestselling snack foods, with nearly half a billion produced each year. The name was coined after the inventor saw a billboard advertising "Twinkle Toe" shoes. The original Twinkie was made with banana cream, but the company switched to vanilla cream due to rationing during World War II. This new flavor became so popular that Twinkies have been made that way ever since.

REASON: A Twinkie is filled with cream and is the same color as the skin tone of the characters on *The Simpsons*, so this would be a great name for Homer's junk. As a name for a real dick, Twinkie has an effeminate and somewhat patronizing ring to it that won't be appreciated.

RATING:

THE WHOPPER

ORIGIN: The Whopper is the centerpiece sandwich at Burger King. It was created in 1957 by the restaurant founder, James McLamore, and originally sold for 37 cents. It costs a lot more than that now, but despite the price hike you can still get it flame grilled and made your way, same as fifty years ago.

REASON: You're lucky if your or your partner's crotch is the home of the Whopper—one big meaty piece of the family jewels.

RATING:

Vehicle Names

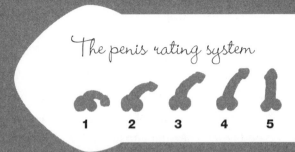

The penis rating system

1 2 3 4 5

This chapter is for penises with real horsepower. Many guys love loud, fast, and powerful driving machines. There's something about being in the driver's seat of a drool-worthy car that gets a guy's blood flowing straight into his crotch. The names in this section reflect the sex connection between guys and their cars, trucks, and motorcycles.

BENTLEY

ORIGIN: The posh Bentley sedan is the vehicle of choice for both royalty and hip-hop stars. It's a powerful symbol of wealth and success, which means wannabes are also found behind the wheel of a Bentley. If a man is driving a Bentley, he may look like a tycoon, but he could just be the chauffeur.

REASON: Yup, turns out that handsome rich guy who picked you up in his amazing car actually stole it. A Bentley's performance in bed mirrors this guy's personality: he looks and acts like he knows what he's doing but the reality is that he's a lemon.

RATING:

EXCALIBUR

ORIGIN: The Excalibur roadster is a popular choice if you want to flash like a Texas oil baron or a cartoon villain. It's, of course, named after the famous sword King Arthur pulled from the stone.

REASON: Many women have tried to pull this sword from its sheath, but few have succeeded. Excalibur is a discriminating penis, but if it's a woman's destiny to lift him up, then she's about to go on a legendary journey that will be told for years to come.

RATING:

HERBIE THE LOVE BUG

ORIGIN: Herbie is the fictional Volkswagen Beetle and star of a long-running series of Disney movies, beginning with *The Love Bug* (1968) and continuing to the latest version,

Herbie: Fully Loaded, from 2005. Herbie is the original smart car: He can drive on his own and "speaks" with his lights and horn.

REASON: A woman has a special relationship with a Herbie penis. Yes, he's cute and lovable, but it's a little weird that she thinks he can speak to her. He's not talking; he's just horny!

RATING:

JETPACK

ORIGIN: The dream of a society where everyone flies around town with a jetpack strapped to their back is sadly packed away along with old comic books and sci-fi novels. Jetpacks exist, but they're so cumbersome and impractical that the only people who use them are nerds with a death wish.

REASON: A Jetpack is dick who likes to take his lover from behind in order to strap onto her back. This position is for real rocketeers only, but it lets the Jetpack lift a lady up off her feet and blast off inside her.

RATING:

MINI COOPER

ORIGIN: The compact Mini Cooper was Britain's equivalent of the VW Bug. It was small and affordable and became a symbol of the swinging sixties. With the Mini's relaunch in the twenty-first century, it has once again become a cool car for a new generation of drivers.

REASON: This little penis is an unsatisfying fit for even the tiniest of parking spaces. Petite girls only need register for this ride.

RATING:

MOON BUGGY

ORIGIN: NASA used lunar rovers—fast manned vehicles driven across the surface of the moon—during three of the Apollo missions in the seventies. Made of lightweight materials, the rovers made it possible for the astronauts to travel across greater distances than in previous missions. Finally, astronauts weren't limited to travel only by foot in their bulky space suits; they could kick back in their buggy, catch some gamma rays, and cruise the moon dunes.

REASON: This Moon Buggy likes to explore lunar bodies with kisses and caresses, and wants nothing more than to probe a woman's heinie. His mission, after all, is to find the dark side of your moon to plant his flag.

RATING:

MUSTANG

ORIGIN: In 1964 Ford released the Mustang, and it quickly became a classic of American cars. New generations of drivers have fallen for the Mustang and its image as a sporty and fun ride.

REASON: An all-American penis, a Mustang is also a sporty and fun ride in the bedroom. It may take some hard work to break this wild stallion, but it will be worth it. Once a woman has tamed him enough to get him into her bed, we recommend that she climb on top of this bucking bronco and hold on tight. Because it is going to be quite the ride!

RATING:

SUBMARINE

ORIGIN: Different versions of submarines, vehicles that are capable of undersea operation without being tied to the surface, were built as early as the nineteenth century, but it wasn't until World War I that subs were put to wider use. Nowadays subs are an integral part of any first-class navy. They also make a delicious lunch.

REASON: A Submarine is long, sleek, and powerful and takes it "victims" by surprise. A woman will be surprised at how controlled this massive member is as it keeps from firing his torpedoes as long as it takes.

RATING:

TANK

ORIGIN: Tanks have been used in warfare since World War I when the British used them to storm over German trenches. They feature a huge-caliber gun set on a rotating turret, which has terrorized enemies and enthralled little boys for decades.

REASON: Some lucky little boys grow up to have armored vehicles in their pants. If you have or want to play with one, climb on board and fire the cannon!

RATING:

VIPER

ORIGIN: The Viper is both a sports car from Dodge that helped return muscle cars to the forefront of American style as well as a venomous snake with a scary set of fangs.

REASON: Power and danger? Those sound like a good mix for a ride around the block on a Viper.

This muscle-bound penis looks threatening but he's actually a gentle cock-cobra. Those are just love bites—nothing to worry about. Just remember to be safe and bring some antivenom.

RATING:

Video Game Names

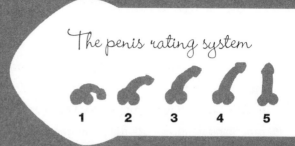

The penis rating system

1 2 3 4 5

It's not just kids anymore that play video games. Nowadays men play out their fantasies on a regular basis by grabbing hold of a joystick and enjoying some digital role-playing. All those hours of practicing hand-eye coordination translates into a dude who knows how to use both his mitts to push all the right buttons for combo moves and power ups under the covers. Use this chapter to find the right name for the dick who likes slipping out of his clothes and into character.

BIG BUCK HUNTER

ORIGIN: Hunting and drinking together has always been fun, but the Big Buck Hunter arcade game finally made shooting animals while drinking booze a safe activity. This game is a favorite for urban bar patrons looking for the thrill of the hunt without having to deal with the mess of dragging a deer carcass home.

REASON: The Big Buck Hunter is a dick on safari for somebody's hide. For this guy, half the fun is in the hunt itself. He loves spotting a beautiful doe-eyed target and having to using his twelve gauge to overcome its defenses.

RATING:

DIG DUG

ORIGIN: Dig Dug is a classic old-school video game from Japan that hit American shores in 1982 on Atari.

The concept of the game is deceptively simple: The player has to direct the character through a series of underground levels and clear each one of monsters and dragons by inflating the monsters with an air pump until they explode. Each board gets progressively harder as more and more beasties appear that need to be popped.

REASON: Dig Dug is a penis that's never happier than when he's burrowing deep underground into his lady. He has seemingly endless energy when it comes to pumping away at her. He'll pump, pump, pump until he blows up.

RATING:

DONKEY KONG

ORIGIN: Donkey Kong is a video game gorilla that first appeared in arcades around the world in 1981. Over the years, Donkey Kong has taken a journey from being a barrel-throwing villain in his first appearance, to seeing the error of his ways and becoming a hero in his latest outings.

REASON: A man with this dick doesn't have to have kidnapped Mario's girlfriend in his younger days. He just needs to be hung like a donkey and as strong as an ape. Ladies, before you know it, you'll be getting it on with a Donkey Kong.

RATING:

DONKEY KONG JR.

ORIGIN: Donkey Kong Jr. is (as you may have guessed) the son of Donkey Kong. The game of the same name was first released in arcades in 1982 as a continuation of the epic saga of the Donkey Kong family. This version flips the script from the original game so that DKJ (that's what the cool kids call him) must rescue his ape daddy, who's been captured by Mario.

REASON: DKJ may be a big ape one day, but for now he's just a young chimp in his twenties. He'll need some time to grow into his mature gorilla suit, but that doesn't mean an older ape can't monkey around with him.

RATING:

FROGGER

ORIGIN: Frogger is a classic video game, as anyone who spent time shelling out quarters at an arcade in the eighties knows. The goal of the game was addictively simple: guide a Frog character across a busy street and over a river while avoiding obstacles like speeding cars and hungry alligators.

REASON: Frogger is a penis that jumps from girl to girl. He loves the thrill of the game and gets a rush out of not getting caught by any jealous girl frogs. Ladies, we don't recommend that you participate in this dick's ongoing game of leap-frog unless you don't mind being left alone on your lily pad in the morning.

RATING: 🍆

GAME BOY

ORIGIN: The Nintendo Game Boy wasn't the only hand-held game console, nor was it the most techno-logically advanced, but despite that it became a monster hit, destroy-ing the competition from Atari and Sega. Its color scheme was limited to green and black, and it had a miniscule screen and tinny sound, but its relatively low cost and won-derfully addictive games made it a must-have. Finally, you could play Tetris on the bus, in bed, or in the back row of math class.

REASON: Some big things do come in small packages. A Game Boy is pocket-sized fun that fits per-fectly in your hand. This dick makes up for his small size with enthusi-asm, and he can—and will—come anywhere you want him to.

RATING: 🍆

GLASS JOE

ORIGIN: Glass Joe's original appearance was in the arcade ver-sion of the classic *Punch-Out!* How-ever, most gamers probably know him as the first-level fighter faced in Nintendo's *Mike Tyson's Punch-Out!* Glass Joe is a glass-jawed boxer who is easily defeated. He's basi-cally a human punching bag that players use as a warm-up for the matches with the game's tougher opponents.

REASON: The dick of a timid, nervous guy earns the dishonor of being called Glass Joe. Women have to handle this overly sensitive cock with kid gloves, so take it easy on him. He may think he's more of a lover than a fighter, but he's really not cut out for either. Women will probably run out of patience trying not to hurt this dick in the bedroom. End the round against Glass Joe with a knockout punch and leave him in the ring.

RATING: 🦴

GUITAR HERO

ORIGIN: The Guitar Hero video game series finally put all those lonely years of playing air guitar in front of your bedroom mirror to good use. Basically karaoke for guitar, a player scores points by pushing the buttons on a plastic toy guitar that corresponds to the notes in a song. Guitar Hero may make you feel like Eric Clapton for a few glorious min-

utes, but your dreams of going on a world tour are staying in your living room.

REASON: Smart guys figure out at an early age that learning some tunes on a guitar is a great way to increase their chances of getting laid. Memorizing the notes to just one Coldplay song can make a boring personality seem "brooding" and make a crappy car appear "retro." How else to explain John Mayer dating women so far above his station? A man with a Guitar Hero will convince his lover that he is a rock star virtuoso when he serenades her with the Fender in his underwear.

RATING: 🦴

LUIGI

ORIGIN: Luigi is Mario's brother, and the character played by the second player in the arcade game Mario

Bros. Players were given a choice of using Luigi as the primary character in the home game system Nintendo Super Mario Bros 2.

REASON: Sometimes women plan out a threesome with two cocks that they choose specifically to be their lovers. But sometimes they end up in a ménage à trois with one alpha cock who they choose for the lead, and the other penis is there in a supporting role. Well, in those cases the *other* dick in a threesome is called Luigi. He's probably just happy to be there and won't mind watching while you get it on with the star of the show. However, you can count on him to rise to the occasion as a backup if necessary.

RATING:

MARIO

ORIGIN: Mario first appeared in the arcade hit Donkey Kong as a carpenter tasked with saving a woman from the clutches of a barrel-tossing ape. Donkey Kong and its sequels were so successful that Nintendo launched a new game starring Mario. The game Mario Bros. turned Mario into a plumber who must travel through a fantasy world in order to save a princess from the evil Bowser. The game was a huge hit and kicked off one of the most enduring series of video games in history, and turned Mario into Nintendo's most famous mascot.

REASON: A man with a Mario treats his lover like a princess. He'll always stand up for her and he's not afraid to get dirty and wet when they're fooling around. This penis will handily plumb the depths of her body.

And by the way, if you're feeling kinky you can invite Mario's brother Luigi over for a game of tag team.

RATING:

MEGA MAN

ORIGIN: MegaMan is Capcom's prolific series of video games. The eponymous hero MegaMan—a robot built to defend the world from a collection of evil robots—made his first appearance on the Nintendo home system in 1987 and immediately became a hit.

REASON: A dude with this penis is such a stud that women often think he's more than human. They wonder if his Mega Man runs on battery power, because he has the stamina of a sex-bot. Have fun plugging in and powering up with this randy machine.

RATING:

PAC-MAN

ORIGIN: The star of this classic video game conquers board after board by chomping on power pellets and avoiding ghosts.

REASON: A Pac-Man is a penis that is very methodical in how he has sex. He pounds away at a girl's power pellet over and over again until he wins the high score. Chomp, chomp, chomp.

RATING:

SONIC

ORIGIN: In 1991 video game maker Sega needed to find a character that could compete with Nintendo's Mario Bros. series of games. Sonic the Hedgehog was born, and ever since he and Mario have been jockeying for the top spot in fans' hearts.

REASON: Porn stars' elder statesman Ron Jeremy is nicknamed "the

Hedgehog," so there is precedence for a lust-filled furry beast. But a man with a Sonic is more than just an animal in the sack. He's a screamer that likes to talk dirty, so you may have to soundproof your bedroom. Cover your ears and get ready to have your sheets blown off by the Sonic boom-boom in your room.

RATING:

Athletic Names

The penis rating system

1 2 3 4 5

Most guys love sports, so it shouldn't be any surprise that so many sports terms have been adapted for sexual language. Touchdowns, home runs, scoring—these are words that guys understand because they capture the competitiveness and the fulfillment of winning that they want in sports on the field and between the sheets. Turns out sports are also a great place to look for penis names too.

AIR JORDAN

ORIGIN: Michael Jordan is widely considered to be the greatest basketball player to ever play the game. His basketball accomplishments include winning two Olympic gold medals and six NBA titles with the Chicago Bulls. His ability to make unbelievable leaps across the court to sink dunks earned him the nickname "Air Jordan."

REASON: A man with an Air Jordan is athletic, successful, and at the top of his game. Is there any question that you should play a little one-on-one with this dick? Just do it!

RATING:

ANDRE THE GIANT

ORIGIN: Professional wrestler Andre the Giant was so big that he was given the nickname "the Eighth Wonder of the World." Andre was a monster in the ring but a quiet and beloved man in real life. Andre was born in France, where he began his career, but gained worldwide fame when he moved to the United States and started wrestling in the WWF. He became the highest-paid wrestler in the league and one of the most well known personalities of the 1980s. Andre's stardom reached a peak when he starred in the film *The Princess Bride* as, what else, a gentle giant.

REASON: Andre the Giant is big—really big. A man with this dick will lavish his lover with affection, because she is his princess and she loves getting "royally screwed."

RATING:

A-ROD

ORIGIN: Alex Rodriguez, aka A-Rod, is a third baseman for the New York Yankees and one of the best all-around players to ever pick up a bat and ball. His records keep stacking up, including being the youngest player to ever hit 500 home runs and having one of the highest-paying contracts in baseball history, but his career has also been marked by controversy.

REASON: An A-Rod is a dick that hits home runs night in and night out. Who cares if he uses performance-enhancing drugs? This guy is a big bat that knows how to swing like a World Series champion.

RATING:

BECKS

ORIGIN: David "Becks" Beckham is the most famous and lauded soccer (excuse me, football) player in the world. He's so famous that he's a household name even in America, where soccer ranks just above volleyball in terms of popularity. Becks became a regular character in the tabloids after his marriage to former member of the Spice Girls Victoria, and he was the focus of Keira Knightley's affection in the movie *Bend It Like Beckham*.

REASON: The athletic Becks has a taste for spicy girls. He'll bend over backwards for his posh lady.

RATING:

BLACK JACK

ORIGIN: "Black" Jack Johnson was an American boxer who became the first black world heavyweight boxing champion in 1908. He was an outspoken man criticized throughout his life for pushing back against the racist conventions of his time. Despite being a well-known public figure, Johnson spent a year in jail for dating a white woman, who eventually became his wife. Johnson successfully fought off James Jeffries in the heavily promoted "Fight of the Century." He was one of the earliest celebrity athletes of modern times, with a reputation for living his life in a way that is de rigueur for today's athletes, such as flaunting his wealth, engaging the media, and product endorsement.

REASON: A man with a Black Jack is tall, dark, handsome, and the undisputed champion of the bedroom. This dick has it all and, once he has a woman down, she won't ever want to get back up.

RATING:

THE GREAT WHITE HOPE

ORIGIN: James J. Jeffries was an American boxer who became the heavyweight-boxing champion of the world in 1899. Jeffries is infamously remembered for returning to the ring out of retirement in 1910 in order to challenge African-American fighter Jack Johnson, the heavyweight champion at the time. Jeffries was billed as the "the Great White Hope" by the media, who played up the racial divide of the country to promote the fight. Jeffries lost to Johnson and never fought professionally again.

REASON: Black men have a reputation for having large penises; there's a reason that women who "go black" never "go back." But when a woman decides to try white meat again, she is looking for her Great White Hope every time the pants come down.

RATING:

HULK HOGAN

ORIGIN: The face of the World Wrestling Federation, Hulk Hogan was a significant factor in the explosion in fame experienced by professional wrestling in the

1980s and 1990s. The Hulk's heroic, all-American image stirred up mainstream Hulkamania across the United States with a Saturday-morning cartoon show, action figures, and TV appearances.

REASON: The Hulk is a dick that gets so turned on when he sees a hot chick that he may turn into a sex maniac and rip right through his shorts.

RATING:

JUNKYARD DOG

ORIGIN: The Junkyard Dog was a WWF wrestler who entered the ring to Queen's "Another One Bites the Dust" and was known for his in-ring antics, which included barking at his opponents and pretending to urinate on defeated foes.

REASON: The Junkyard Dog is a dirty boy in the bedroom, but he's just looking for a dirty girl who can train him to roll over and beg for her treats.

RATING:

THE ROCK

ORIGIN: Dwayne Johnson is a famous actor now, but he first gained fame as the professional wrestler "the Rock." The Rock's quirks included referring to himself in the third-person and conducting comedic interviews that became fan favorites. He was a charismatic and popular wrestler, despite frequently acting the role of a villain, who nicknamed himself "the people's Champion."

REASON: A penis called the Rock says, "I am as hard as stone." Ladies, put on your rock-climbing gear and mount this Mountain Man.

RATING:

WILT CHAMBERLAIN

ORIGIN: Wilt Chamberlain is one of the greatest basketball players to have played the game. Nicknames like "Wilt the Stilt" and "the Big Dipper" hint at the physically dominating natural abilities that Wilt had, which led to MVP awards, record titles, and induction into the NBA Hall of Fame. Wilt was also a notorious ladies' man who claimed to have slept with 20,000 women in his lifetime, which if true would mean that he had sex at the unbelievable rate of about eight women per week from age fifteen to his death at age sixty-three.

REASON: A cock named Wilt Chamberlain is a champion player whose scoring records have reached mythical status. This dick didn't just master the game; he reinvented it.

Men want their penises to be just like him, and women are just waiting for their turn to be with him.

RATING:

Toy-Inspired Names

The penis rating system

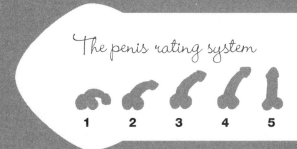

1 2 3 4 5

If your favorite plaything is a penis, why not name it after a toy? You'll feel like a kid again when you spend hours and hours giving and receiving pleasure on your own or with a group. But you don't have to go to a store to find this toy, and you won't get bored with it after a few hours of playing around. This toy is endless fun, and the first game to play is finding a name, so let's roll those dice!

BATTLESHIP

ORIGIN: The heavily armed battleship was the symbol of naval dominance through both World Wars and for much of the twentieth century. However, with the advent of long-range aircraft and guided missiles, battleships became irrelevant and were slowly replaced with destroyers and aircraft carriers. The last battleship was taken out of commission by the U.S. Navy in 2006, which means the only active battleship wars originate from game maker Milton Bradley, which has been producing a version of the game of Battleship since 1943.

REASON: This penis has the heavy caliber of a navy warship and is just as contentious as a game of Battleship. The sex is fantastic, even though this dick's lover is always fighting for supremacy over the relationship. She'll probably find that the fights are worth having when this guy sinks his battleship into her ocean.

RATING:

BOOMERANG

ORIGIN: Throwing sticks have been used for sport and hunting and as weapons by a variety of ancient civilizations around the world for tens of thousands of years, but the Aborigines of Australia are most well known for creating the returning boomerang. The boomerang is a curved pieced of wood shaped in such a way that a skilled thrower can use it to accurately hit a target hundreds of meters away, and if he misses his mark, it will come flying back into his hands.

REASON: A Boomerang is a dick that keeps coming back for more. Depending on what type of cock he is, this could be a good or bad thing. On one hand, if the sex is great and he keeps coming back, you've got him under your spell. On the other hand, if he's a creep, you want this Boomerang out of your hands as quickly as possible before he becomes a repeat offender that you can't get rid of.

RATING: 🍑 OR 🍆

LINCOLN LOG

ORIGIN: This toy made log cabin architects out of all of us. Partly inspired by the childhood home of Abraham Lincoln, the miniature wooden logs interlock, making it possible to build relatively stable little buildings, depending on one's patience following instructions. A cool fact about Lincoln Logs is that the son of famous architect Frank Lloyd Wright created them. And Frank Lloyd Wright's original middle name? Lincoln. Guess he

thought Lloyd would attract the ladies?

REASON: The Lincoln Log is so big and hard you could build a house with it. The lucky lumberjack with this hard wood can lay some timber. The Lincoln Log wields the Panty Emancipation Proclamation, which will separate a girl from her underwear.

RATING: 🍆

MR. MONOPOLY

ORIGIN: Monopoly is the most-played board game in the world; you might say that Monopoly has a monopoly on board games. The rules are simple: buy up all the properties and earn the most money and you will be the winner. And, oh yeah, stay out of jail.

REASON: Mr. Monopoly may not wear a top hat and tux, but like his namesake, this penis wants everything for himself, including his woman. It might be possible to tolerate this greedy attitude for a while, but not if the thing in his pants is the size of a game piece. If this is the case, run, don't walk, past "Go" and find a new playmate.

RATING:

MR. POTATO HEAD

ORIGIN: Mr. Potato Head holds the honor of being the first toy to have a TV commercial. It revolutionized how toys were sold to kids, and parents have had to listen to cries of "buy me that or I'll die!" ever since. The original Mr. Potato Head was sold as a bunch of body parts meant to be stuck in an actual potato or other vegetable; the plastic body didn't arrive until years later. The most fun part of Mr. Potato Head is that any of his parts can be stuck in any of his holes, so you can create a face that would make Picasso proud.

REASON: The name Mr. Potato Head goes to the dick who tries to slide into a woman's ear, nose, or in any other inappropriate place on her face. He actually thinks that she gets turned on by having his tater tots slapped in her face. This stupid spud will keep sticking his French fry in all the wrong places until she threatens to get the potato peeler from the kitchen.

RATING:

NERF

ORIGIN: In 1969 the first orange foam NERF (Non-Expanding Recreational Foam) ball appeared and made it possible to throw a ball inside the house without pissing off your mom. The ever-growing line of soft balls, darts, and discs has become a mainstay in households worldwide.

REASON: A Nerf penis is safe to play with, but that's because it's always soft. You won't get hurt, but if you don't find another type of toy you might die of boredom.

RATING:

PLAY-DOH

ORIGIN: Play-Doh has become a ubiquitous part of every kindergarten and playroom, but its invention as a toy was a happy accident. Originally made as a wallpaper cleaner, the manufacturer started marketing it as colorful molding clay after he discovered that schoolchildren were using leftover stuff to make Christmas ornaments.

REASON: This name is for a doughy dick that's fun to play with. Ladies, don't fret that he might be a bit soft in the middle. Play-Doh is always putty in your hands.

RATING:

RAGGEDY ANDY

ORIGIN: Raggedy Andy was created in 1920 as the brother to Raggedy Ann, a doll that was first made for the creator's daughter, and then starred in the book *Raggedy Ann Stories*. The Raggedys are celebrity siblings of the toy world, having appeared in dozens of illustrated children's books, an animated TV series, and of course as dolls.

REASON: Raggedy Andy's owner wears unkempt, shabby clothes, but that somehow makes this penis even cuter. He makes any woman want to take him home, clean him up, and treat him like her rag doll.

RATING:

ROCK 'EM SOCK 'EM ROBOT

ORIGIN: Rock 'Em Sock 'Em Robots is a two-player toy boxing game. Each player chooses either a red or blue plastic robot fighter and uses a joystick to punch the other. The one who strikes a direct hit to his opponent will pop its head off its body and win the match.

REASON: When the Rock 'Em Sock 'Em Robot goes "pop" in a ladiy's mouth it might seem like her head will get knocked off, but don't worry, she can take it. Ladies, prepare to have your socks rocked off and enjoy having a tussle under the covers.

RATING:

SHRINKY DINK

ORIGIN: Just about every kid who grew up in the eighties played with Shrinky Dinks at some point. You'd just choose a cartoon pattern on a thin piece of plastic, stick it in the oven, and watch it shrink into a hard, little figurine. Then video games were invented, after which kids only came back to the kitchen to grab snacks in between rounds of Space Invaders.

REASON: The Shrinky Dink dick is a rare find. Most penises grow in size from some stimulation, but the Shrinky Dink actually gets *smaller* when it's near sexual heat. It's the incredible shrinking dinkus!

RATING:

SLINKY

ORIGIN: The Slinky toy was a happy accident discovered by an army engineer when he knocked a spring off a shelf and watched it "walk" from shelf to floor. Slinkies have been brought into space, have been used to make music, and were named the official state toy of Pennsylvania.

REASON: He might sound like a shady guy creeping in the shadows, but a guy with a Slinky really earns his name from the yoga-like mastery over his limber dick. His ability to bend over backwards makes all those hard-to-reach positions in the last chapter of the *Kamasutra* possible. Plus, just like its toy namesake, a Slinky is flexible enough to go either way. After all, as the jingle says, Slinky is a wonderful toy, and it's fun for a girl or a boy!

RATING:

TRIVIAL PURSUIT

ORIGIN: Trivial Pursuit is a game that is played by moving around a board and correctly answering questions in six distinct categories of general knowledge. Certain spaces on the board award a right answer with a little wedge. The first person to earn wedges in each category wins the game. The person with the most useless knowledge—and a little luck—wins the game.

REASON: This is a hard-to-get cock that a woman and her friends compete for, just for the hell of it. Chasing after some guy's Trivial Pursuit might be meaningless fun just to pass the time, but you'll feel a little pride by winning a slice of him.

RATING:

WIFFLE BALL BAT

ORIGIN: The Wiffle Ball was invented in 1953 by a father who wanted to give his twelve-year-old son a new type of backyard ball that would curve easily. The ball was paired up with a yellow, lightweight plastic bat that's easy for anyone to use. The inventor's son loved the new game, and named it "whiff," after the sound the bat made when a player swings a strike. Dads have been whiffing their son's pitches ever since.

REASON: A guy playing with a kiddie toy like a Wiffle Ball Bat is going to be stuck playing with himself in the backyard. Forget about coming into home, he's lucky to get on first base. This amateur player strikes out every time.

RATING:

YO-YO

ORIGIN: The earliest surviving yo-yo dates back to Greece, 500 B.C. Artifacts have been discovered of ancient toy disks made from terra cotta, wood, or metal attached to string. The yo-yo seems to be a toy with near-universal existence. Evidence of early yo-yos has been found in civilizations as far-flung as those of the ancient Chinese, Mayans, and Egyptians. It's not impossible to imagine a young King Tut performing the "walk the dog" trick to impress girls along the banks of the Nile.

REASON: Ladies, don't let this name fool you. The guy with a Yo-Yo isn't playing around with a toy. He has mastery over his speed and movements in order to dip in and out of his lover again and again without losing control. The Yo-Yo master knows enough head-spinning tricks to keep a woman coming back over and over.

RATING:

Ad Icon Names

The penis rating system

1 2 3 4 5

Brand mascots are used to sell us cereal, frozen vegetables, and batteries, so why not use one to find a name for a beloved dick? A successful mascot transcends the product it's selling to represent something more than itself, becoming an idea that elicits emotion of its own. Grownups everywhere hold a special place in their heart for the silly rabbit or lucky leprechaun that smiled at them from the box of their favorite cereal, while generations of consumers have had a love/hate relationship with the Marlboro Man. The names in this chapter tap into the emotional resonance that some of the most well known advertising icons have created.

CAP'N CRUNCH

ORIGIN: Cap'n Crunch was created in the early 1960s, during a time when kids' cereals were flourishing, and for some reason it made sense that a cartoon naval captain would sell a breakfast food. The woman who developed the taste of the cereal based it on a recipe her grandma made. Another cool fact is that the animator who created *Rocky and Bullwinkle*, Jay Ward, also created the Cap'n Crunch character.

REASON: Cap'n Crunch is a penis that belongs to a hippie ("crunchy," as in crunchy granola). A diet of organic fruits and nuts from the local co-op, never a mass-market breakfast cereal, keeps this Cap'n healthy and ready to sail the sexual seas at all times.

RATING:

CRACKER JACK

ORIGIN: Cracker Jack's combination of caramel-coated popcorn mixed with peanuts has been an American snack staple since the 1893 World's Fair. It's name came when a first-time customer declared, "This is cracker [meaning "great"], jack [slang for "man"]!" It has been so intertwined with our great American pastime (baseball) that the song "Take Me Out to the Ballgame," with the lyric "buy me some peanuts and Cracker Jack" is traditionally sung during the seventh-inning stretch.

REASON: A Cracker Jack is a cock that a girl can't stuff in her mouth fast enough. A sweet 'n' salty dick never tasted this good.

RATING:

ENERGIZER BUNNY

ORIGIN: The Energizer Bunny, the unstoppable pink toy rabbit wearing sunglasses and beating a bass drum, was originally created as a satire of Energizer's rival battery manufacturer Duracell. But the bunny mascot has become so ingrained in our culture that he's become symbolic of an indomitable spirit, used by everyone from politicians to star athletes to describe their gutsiness.

REASON: The Energizer Bunny is a nonstop sex machine. It's unclear what gives this dick such superior endurance, but it's more than just carrots. You won't get any sleep when you spend the night in this bunny's hutch. He keeps going and going and going. . . .

RATING:

JOE CAMEL

ORIGIN: Today's youngsters may be surprised to learn that there was a time not too long ago when one of the tobacco industry's most popular mascots was a cartoon camel named Joe. The makers of Camel cigarettes insisted that the character wasn't meant to attract kids to smoking, but their argument didn't hold much water considering that he looked like the star of an animated Saturday-morning series that just happens to love cooling out with a smoke.

REASON: At first look a Joe Camel dick will appear to be a stud, but closer inspection reveals that he's just a mirage. This cock has a funky quirk. Like the desert native he's named after, he likes to dry hump. Like a virgin attempting his first quasi-sexual experience, Joe Camel will fumblingly rub against his lover, make a mess in his pants, and leave her unsatisfied.

RATING:

THE JOLLY GREEN GIANT

ORIGIN: As the smiling protector of canned peas, the Jolly Green Giant has been scaring kids into eating their veggies since 1925. He's like the Gandhi of giants, contradicting the common bias that all giants want to terrorize the countryside and grind people's bones to make their bread.

REASON: A Jolly Green Giant is a larger-than-life cock. He is always ready to party. A girl doesn't have to feel bad about being his "Ho, Ho, Ho" for a while and enjoying his greenery.

RATING:

THE KING

ORIGIN: Burger King's "King" has the honor of being the creepiest mascot ever to sell fast food. Sure, some people are scared of clowns and may not appreciate Ronald McDonald, but the King's masked face has done the unthinkable: successfully synthesize serial killer imagery with cheeseburgers. The King is disturbing, but you have to respect an ad that can sell a product while causing nightmares.

REASON: It's been said before, but that's because it's true: It's good to be the king. This King is no dictator in the bedroom, however. He's a gracious boner, and he always insists that a woman has it her way, right away.

RATING:

KOOL AID MAN

ORIGIN: Kool-Aid Man is the Pitcher Man pitchman for Kool-Aid. In the commercials, when a kid shouts "Hey Kool-Aid!" Kool-Aid Man crashes through a wall, shouting "Oh yeah!" in return, and he delivers a tasty red drink to the thirsty girls and boys. He's been leaving giant pitcher-shaped holes in walls for decades.

REASON: A Kool Aid Man belongs to a guy who is big enough to run through a wall, but is also the coolest dude around. This dude is so smooth he'll have some lucky lady drinking his Kool Aid soon enough.

RATING:

MARLBORO MAN

ORIGIN: It's hard to imagine it now, but Marlboro cigarettes were originally marketed exclusively to women, and sales were bad. Phillip Morris had to figure out a way to sell their flagging filtered cigarette, considered feminine at the time, to men who were starting to realize that smoking might not be the healthiest habit. The answer was creating a mascot that sold the image of strong, masculine independence. Thus, the Marlboro Man was born: a rugged cowboy riding the range, herding cattle, and of course, smoking a Marlboro. Lung cancer never looked so badass.

REASON: A guy doesn't need a pack-a-day smoking habit to have a Marlboro Man. But his dick does have to be a tough, all-American stud. Even if a girl swore to never smoke a ciggie in her life, she won't mind lighting one up with this cowboy.

RATING:

MR. CLEAN

ORIGIN: Mr. Clean is the brand name of Procter & Gamble's line of cleaning products, as well as the name of the brand's muscle-bound and shiny-headed mascot. Mr. Clean must have had a strong effect on 1950s'-era housewives left at home while their husbands commuted into the city to work corporate jobs because within six months of his introduction it became the bestselling cleaner in America. Once Ward, Wally, and the Beave left the house, June Cleaver and Donna Reed were home fantasizing about a guy in a tight white shirt with a gold earring.

REASON: A dude with a Mr. Clean will give his lover a bath to scrub all her dirty places before making sweet love to her. He'll also leave the house spic and span while she sleeps off the cleaning his Mr. Clean gave her plumbing the night before.

RATING:

MR. GOODWRENCH

ORIGIN: Everybody dreads that moment when their car breaks down, because it often means a trip to the mechanic that will ravage their wallets. Mechanics have a bad reputation for gouging customers who know very little about cars yet have no choice but to pay exorbitant fees to get their ride back on the road. General Motors recognized peoples' mechanic-anxiety, so they began a campaign featuring Mr. Goodwrench, a knowledgeable, honest, and friendly mechanic who can only be found at GM repair shops.

REASON: Mr. Goodwrench belongs to a dude who knows how to properly use his tool. This dick can rotate you, tighten you, or loosen you up, without ever losing his firm grip.

RATING:

MR. PEANUT

ORIGIN: Mr. Peanut was created in 1916 by a schoolboy, who won a contest to create a logo for Planters Nuts. The winning logo was a nut with human features but an artist later added the distinctive top hat, cane, and monocle that give Mr. Peanut so much class.

REASON: If a man has a penis the size of a peanut hanging from his crotch, you may have to question whether he's a man at all. This guy's Mr. Peanut might get salty from being rejected, but that's his problem.

RATING:

THE PILLSBURY DOUGHBOY

ORIGIN: The Pillsbury Doughboy has been selling pancake mix and crescent rolls since 1965. "Dough-boy" is actually a job title; the given name of the anthropomorphic boy made of dough is officially "Poppin' Fresh." He wears a baker's hat and scarf, which indicates that Poppin' Fresh is a baker himself. Besides the implicit danger in being made of dough and working around hot ovens, it's disturbing to consider the ethical implications of a boy made of dough making and selling baked goods. Oh well, at least the rolls are delicious.

REASON: The Doughboy—or Poppin' if you're nasty—is a sweet dick that giggles when you poke his doughy underbelly. The guy attached to this penis is also a fantastic baker, which explains why he's such a softy. Ladies, if you love fresh cookies after sex and don't mind a few extra calories, this is the guy for you.

RATING: 🍆

QUAKER MAN

ORIGIN: Despite popular misconception, the Quaker Oats man isn't Pennsylvania-founder William Penn. He's just a generic guy who happens to look like an old man in colonial drag. The founders of the cereal brand used the Quaker as their symbol because the Quaker faith represents integrity, honesty, and purity. It also promises to keep you regular.

REASON: A Quaker Man belongs to a straight-edge guy who doesn't smoke or drink but thankfully has no hang-ups about sex. In fact, the Quaker Man pursues lovemaking with religious passion and loves

to bone like a teenager let loose on rumspringa. Oh wait, that's the Amish—but you know what we mean!

RATING: 🍆

SMOKEY THE BEAR

ORIGIN: The forests of the American West were especially susceptible to wildfires during World War II because most of the able-bodied men were overseas. The lack of manpower meant that the U.S. Forest Service needed a mascot for their campaign to educate people on fire prevention. Walt Disney lent the character Bambi to the campaign, but after a year a new mascot was needed. Smokey the Bear was chosen, and he's been letting everyone know that "Only you can prevent forest fires!" for over sixty-five years.

REASON: Smokey the Bear burns up the sheets, so keep a fire extinguisher next to the bed. This burly penis performs best when he's tucked away in his cave with his lover. When you find a Smokey the Bear, you'll want to hibernate in bed all winter long.

RATING:

SPUDS MACKENZIE

ORIGIN: Spuds MacKenzie was a bull terrier who was the mascot for Bud Light in the late eighties. Spuds could surf, skateboard, and play guitar, and he was always surrounded by beautiful women. Spuds premiered during a commercial break during the 1987 Super Bowl, and he became an instant hit with audiences, spawning a merchandising empire of T-shirts, toys, and beer cozies.

REASON: Spuds is criticized for being such a dog, but what do you expect from the original party animal? After all, not many dicks have the skill to successfully juggle three women and pilot a yacht while drinking a beer.

RATING:

TONY THE TIGER

ORIGIN: Tony the Tiger has been the mascot for Kellogg's Frosted Flakes since the cereal was introduced almost sixty years ago. Tigers and sugary corn cereal have nothing in common, but when cereal ad men were looking for mascots, they pretty much just ran down a list of zoo animals and made choices at random.

REASON: This cock is a tony lover? He's *gr-r-reat!* Just try and tame this wild tiger.

RATING:

TRIX RABBIT

ORIGIN: The Trix Rabbit has been trying to eat fruity Trix since 1959 when he was introduced as the mascot for the new cereal. Over the years the rabbit has received his own bowl of Trix on rare occasions.

REASON: A Trix Rabbit dick belongs to a creep who tries to sleep with high-school kids. Listen up Rabbit, Trix are for kids! Wait a couple years until they're in college, and then you can have all the Trix you want.

RATING:

Landmark Names

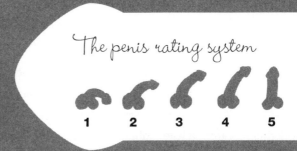

The penis rating system

1 2 3 4 5

The landmarks listed in this chapter have stood the test of time, so a name from this section is perfect for a penis that is just as memorable. Like a souvenir from a fantastic trip, a dick may be the only memory from a wild night of passion in a foreign country with a dark-eyed stranger who speaks another language.

BIG BEN

ORIGIN: Big Ben is the name of the bell that resides in the clock at the top of the tower at the Palace of Westminster in England, but the name is generally used to describe the tower itself. Big Ben is the largest four-faced chiming clock in the world, and is renowned for its reliability, as evidenced by the fact that it continued to run accurately throughout the German Blitz of World War II.

REASON: The Big Ben is a cock that is erect every hour on the hour. This dick is so reliably horny that you can set your watch to his morning wood.

RATING: 🍆

EIFFEL TOWER

ORIGIN: Built as the entrance gate to the 1889 World's Fair, the tower is the tallest building in Paris and the internationally recognized symbol of France. The engineer who designed the tower, Gustave Eiffel, was also the designer of the Statue of Liberty in New York Harbor.

REASON: The Eiffel Tower, aka the French Tickler, belongs to a francophone lover with an *eye-full* in his pants. It's obvious why everyone wants to French kiss this penis.

RATING: 🍆

EMPIRE STATE BUILDING

ORIGIN: The Empire State Building is probably New York City's most famous landmark, and one of the most well known structures in the world. It is renowned for its magnificent art-deco architecture. Getting to the top of its 102 stories should be on the to-do list for any newcomer to NYC: men, women, and giant plane-swatting gorillas included.

REASON: The ESB is the biggest cock in New York City. NYC has a lot of big dicks, and new ones arrive daily, so this is a significant achievement. And just like every true New Yorker, this cock has big, brassy balls.

RATING:

THE GREAT PYRAMID

ORIGIN: The ancient Egyptians built the pyramids as massive tombs to hold the remains of their dead pharaohs. The pyramid at Giza is believed to have been built for the Pharaoh Khufu. It is the oldest, and the only surviving, of the Seven Wonders of the Ancient World. It was the largest man-made structure for 3,800 years. The construction of the building is so spectacular that

it's no wonder aliens have been deemed responsible for it.

REASON: The Great Pyramid dick has a thick base that tapers into a thin head at the tip. Whoever opens the pants and pulls out this penis will be cursed.

RATING:

LEANING TOWER

ORIGIN: The world has numerous leaning towers, but the most famous one is located in Pisa in Italy. Some towers are purposefully built with a lean, but Pisa's most famous building leans as a result of poor construction of the foundation, which is built upon loose soil. The tower continued to slowly droop until it was stabilized into its current fixed, off-kilter position in 2001.

REASON: The Leaning Tower of Penis is a long dick that sticks out at an angle. The owner of this penis has nothing to be ashamed of though, because only significantly large members are so heavy that they tilt to the side.

RATING:

OLD FAITHFUL

ORIGIN: Yellowstone National Park is home to Old Faithful, America's most famous geyser. Old Faithful erupts quite predictably, shooting thousands of gallons of boiling water over a hundred feet in the air about once every hour. In the years following Yellowstone's designation as a National Park, the U.S. Military oversaw its protection. Soldiers used Old Faithful to steam their clothes, like an all-natural laundry service.

REASON: Old Faithful belongs to a mature dude who uses Viagra to keep his geysers "regular." This dick blows on a timely basis about an hour after taking his little blue pill,

which would be right after he pays the dinner check, so make sure you get home and get to bed in time.

RATING:

SEARS TOWER

ORIGIN: Chicago's Sears Tower still stands as the tallest building in the Americas. Construction was paid for fully by the Sears Roebuck Company—the world's largest retailer at the time—who desired a new building to consolidate its huge staff. The Sears Tower was officially renamed the Willis Tower in 2009 when new owners took over the building.

REASON: In honor of Sears's historic place among retailers, the Sears Tower name goes to a long dick enhanced via surgery or bought via pills from a late-night infomercial.

RATING:

THE SPHINX

ORIGIN: The Great Sphinx of Giza is one of the world's largest and oldest statues, yet many questions still surround its origin. Historians disagree over who built the massive limestone statue with the body of a lion and the head of a man and whether it was built in honor of the Nile, the Sun, or perhaps even the stars. Who knows: Maybe some ancient Egyptian queen built it in honor of her man-beast lover.

REASON: The Sphinx is a conundrum, you might say. Women aren't sure why they're so into him and how he always ends up in their bed, but there's something about him that is intriguing nonetheless. He's a puzzle to figure out, and if it will take one more romp in the hay to get closer to the answer, then so be it.

RATING:

STATUE OF LIBERTY

ORIGIN: The Statue of Liberty was a gift from the people of France to the United States in honor of the friendship that was established between the countries during the American Revolution. Its perch on Liberty Island in New York Harbor means that it was frequently the first sight of America viewed by immigrants arriving in their new country. Naturally, the French's gift to us is a woman ready to party; why else would she be wearing a toga?

REASON: The Statue of Liberty is the penis you go to after breaking up with a horrible boyfriend. This dick represents life, liberty, and the pursuit of happiness. Lovers flock to the Statue of Liberty to celebrate their newfound freedom and rejoice in the sexual heat of their new flame.

RATINGS:

TAJ MAHAL

ORIGIN: India's Taj Mahal is the world's finest example of a type of architecture that combines Indian, Persian, and Islamic styles. The Taj was built by an emperor as a mausoleum in honor of his favorite wife.

REASON: The Taj Mahal penis is forever pining for his long-lost love. He'll never get over his ex. You'll know you've had the misfortune of finding this type of penis when the pants come off and you see his last girlfriend's name tattooed on his shaft.

RATING:

Weapon-Inspired Names

The penis rating system

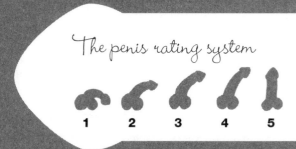

1   2   3   4   5

Just like a penis, it's not the weapon that causes good or bad, it's the person who uses it. Through life you'll encounter every range of penis from BB guns to love rockets, and it's recommended you get as much hands-on training with as many penises as you can find. Support your right to bear arms by grabbing onto a cock and pulling its trigger. But be careful! You have to be a responsible penis owner and make sure that dick doesn't discharge in your face. Use this chapter to hunt down the perfect ammunition for your Saturday-night special.

AK-47

ORIGIN: The AK-47 is an automatic machine gun that was first developed by the Soviet Union in the years following World War II. Though it's not very accurate, it is highly durable and relatively cheap and easy to use, which explains why it is still the most commonly manufactured automatic weapon in the world, six decades after it was first created. Nine out of ten terrorists who bought them on the black market agree it's awesome!

REASON: The AK-47 is cheap, inaccurate, and all too common. This inexperienced penis is found all over the meat markets of big cities, so buyer beware and put this guy back on the shelf before you purchase his merchandise.

RATING: 🌀

BAZOOKA

ORIGIN: The bazooka is a portable rocket launcher invented by the United States to fight tanks during World War II. The stovepipe-shaped bazooka's armor-piercing capability and mobility gave infantry units a previously unavailable advantage in fighting armored vehicles and destroying enemy bunkers. The bazooka's distinctive name is credited to the unique noise the weapon makes during use, but the name has been generalized to refer to any hand-held rocket launcher. The bazooka Joe's were credited for being one of the essential elements that won the war for the Allies.

REASON: A guy with a Bazooka doesn't come quietly. He finishes off with a big, noisy, sweaty explosion. A Bazooka is not recommended for outdoor use, because all his owner's yelling and screaming might scare the neighbors.

RATING:

CATAPULT

ORIGIN: Catapults are mechanical devices that have been used since the time of the ancient Greeks and Romans to hurl objects great heights and distances. Primarily used in siege warfare to overcome the walled defenses of a fortress or castle, these weapons were used throughout the Middle Ages, until they were made obsolete by the invention of gunpowder. Catapults were commonly used to toss stones or large arrows, but sometimes an inventive general would send a diseased animal carcass or rotten garbage over a wall as a form of early biological warfare. Those poor medieval peasants; if they weren't being taxed to death by the local evil sheriff they were defending themselves from raining sewage.

REASON: A penis with the capacity to shoot its load across the room deserves to be called a catapult. A guy who can arc his orgasm like an Olympic shot-putter is rare and should be admired. Ladies, if you find one of these men, test his skill by seeing how accurately he can launch his love bomb onto a target drawn on your body.

RATING:

KATANA

ORIGIN: A katana is a curved Japanese sword. In Japanese *katana* could refer to a single-edged sword, but in general usage outside of Japan the word has come to specifically mean a samurai sword. The katana is renowned for being an especially sharp and lightning-fast weapon in the hands of a master swordsman. Making a katana takes weeks to complete and requires the skills of someone who is both technically adept and has an artist's eye. There may no longer be any true samurai left in the world, but a katana displayed on a mantel is a good way to pretend they still exist.

REASON: Katana is a fitting name for the love-blade of a Japanese paramour or for any man worthy of being called a sexual samurai, regardless of his roots.

RATING: █

LONG SWORD

ORIGIN: The long sword is a meter-long double-edged sword that was used in Europe during the Middle Ages and Renaissance. Due to the large size of these weapons, they typically required two hands to wield and were useful when attacking enemies wearing heavy armor. Nowadays guys buy a big SUV, but back in the old days, knights would display their manhood by swinging around the longest sword they could find at the blacksmith.

REASON: A penis that is so big that you need to use both hands to get a solid grip on it is a Long Sword. Fortunately, this Long Sword is a blunt instrument, so you don't have to worry about cutting yourself on it, but this is still a serious weapon recommended only for those with experience on the battlefield of love.

RATING: █

MUSKET

ORIGIN: A musket is a muzzle-loaded long gun that was created in medieval China and further developed for European and American warfare (think the Three Musketeers and the Minutemen). Loading the musket was an arduous and dangerous process that required multiple steps to load a lead musket ball and a cartridge of loose gunpowder. The most experienced musketeers could fire at a rate of four shots per minute. Individual muskets were inaccurate, so musketeers would form a line to deliver a volley of gunfire like a group shotgun.

REASON: Today's Musket is a leftover from an older, more civilized time. He's an old dick that takes a while to shoot his load and takes so much time to reload that a woman can take a nap between rounds.

Sometimes experience just doesn't compensate for youth.

RATING: 🥾

PATRIOT MISSILE

ORIGIN: The Patriot is an American surface-to-air missile system. The Patriot can shoot down aircraft, but its primary purpose is to intercept enemy missiles. The Patriot became a popular symbol of American power during the Gulf War by protecting the United States and its allies from Iraqi Scud missiles.

REASON: The Patriot Missile is no minuteman. This dick is a proud fighter for love whose flagpole rises every morning like clockwork. He'll sing the National Anthem for a pole polishing.

RATING: 🥾

REVOLVER

ORIGIN: The first firearms had to be reloaded after each shot, a time-consuming and potentially deadly delay that exposed the gunner to enemy attack. The revolver was a significant advancement in hand-held weapons because of its revolving chamber that would quickly rotate and reload with a single pull of the hammer. Lucky for Western fans, because a shootout at high noon would take twenty minutes if gunslingers had to reload muskets.

REASON: The Revolver is quick on the draw, so he'll pull out and fire super-fast, but he's packing a six-shooter, so he'll be ready to go again immediately for a few more rounds.

RATING:

SNIPER RIFLE

ORIGIN: The sniper rifle is for extremely accurate and deadly attacks from long distances. A small force of skilled snipers can turn the tide against a much larger army. Patriot snipers in the American Revolution played a key role in the war by targeting British officers and cutting their leadership off at the head.

REASON: The Sniper slips in, takes down his prey, and just as quickly slides out and away with barely a sound. His attacks can be deadly, so it's recommended that protection is taken; condoms, bulletproof vest, or whatever's handy.

RATING:

STILETTO

ORIGIN: A stiletto is a long, thin dagger with a sharp point used for stabbing. Though quite sharp, their lack of an edge made them a poor cutting weapon. As such, knights often used them to deliver the final blow to an injured opponent, since they could slip through any gaps in an enemy's armor.

REASON: Like its namesake, a stiletto dick is long and thin. A stiletto will usually try to stab you in the back like an ass-assin, so keep your eye on this villain.

RATING:

TOMAHAWK

ORIGIN: The tomahawk is a single-handed ax used by Native Americans as a general-use tool as well as a weapon. A tomahawk can be thrown or used in hand-to-hand combat. American history tells of some gruesome accounts where tomahawks were used to scalp enemies as a symbol of conquest.

REASON: A Tomahawk dick collects blowjobs like trophies. It's been known to nearly take the top of a head off, so women may want to wear a helmet before they become this scalper's prize.

RATING:

TRIDENT

ORIGIN: A trident is a three-pronged spear, originally used by fisherman. Think of it as a nautical pitchfork. A class of Roman gladiators who were designed to look like a group of warrior fishermen specialized in fighting with a trident and net. The trident is also a symbol of Poseidon, and statues of the god commonly show him holding one to represent his dominion over the seas. In modern times the trident is most likely to refer to a type of chewing gum that holds its flavor for approximately thirty seconds.

REASON: The Trident specializes in waterborne sex. He can be found fishing for his prey in hot tubs, swimming pools, and Cancun during spring break. Water-based sex requires balance, advanced doggy-paddling skills, and preferably a lifeguard's license—which this dick just so happens to have.

RATING:

Superhero and Villain Names

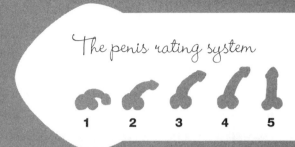

The penis rating system

1 2 3 4 5

Is this penis a Super-cock or just a Joker? Animated action heroes have lots of attitude that translates into a great name. Perhaps naming a dick after a superhero will imbue it with a mutant power, like ESP. A cock that can read your mind? That sounds far-fetched, but a great dick sure can make you feel like you're flying.

BATMAN

ORIGIN: Batman is different from most other superheroes, because he doesn't have any special powers of flight or strength. He's just a smart, tough guy with a cool outfit. But he does have a utility belt full of cool tools and devices that he uses to fight crime.

REASON: A Batman in the bedroom is a special "tool" that isn't afraid to supplement its skills with a variety of devices and toys to make sure he gets you off. A dude with this dick isn't intimidated by battery-powered assistance. He gets more turned on by the more devices you let him use on you.

RATING:

BLACK PANTHER

ORIGIN: The Black Panther was one of the comic-book world's first black superheroes, and one of its sexiest. He is the prince of an African kingdom by day, and a crime fighter by night.

REASON: This is the name for a dark-skinned penis that is an animal in the sack. But the Black Panther doesn't belong to someone who is just a sex machine. This guy will also treat his lady like his queen-to-be.

RATING:

BLADE

ORIGIN: This comic-book hero is probably best known from his onscreen portrayal via Wesley Snipes. He is a half-human, half-vampire vampire hunter with super-human strength, and he is immune to a vampire's bite. He gained his abilities when his mother was bitten by a vampire when pregnant with him.

REASON: A man with this dick is one confused guy. He doesn't know if he should drive his Blade into his lover or bite her neck. Getting staked by a Blade isn't worth the trouble, so send him back to his crypt.

RATING:

BRAINIAC

ORIGIN: The super-smart supervillain Brainiac has been one of Superman's principal enemies since the 1950s. He's a green-skinned alien android whose original MO was traveling through the universe and stealing a planet's knowledge before destroying it. But now his main mission is trying to kill the man in red and blue tights.

REASON: What makes this penis such a genius is that he knows that it takes more than just a dick to get laid. He lets the brain do the work so he gets to enjoy the action. This smarty-pants uses his big sexy brain and charming wit to turn his lucky lady into a smarty-no-pants.

RATING:

CAPTAIN AMERICA

ORIGIN: Captain America stands for the American dream: life, liberty, and the pursuit of happiness. As a superhero he suits up in red, white, and blue tights with his indestructible shield to fight Nazis and Commies in defense of Lady Liberty.

REASON: This man's good looks, strong body, and tough spirit make him the ideal all-American guy. Like any good and horny red-blooded American male, the thought of a patriotic woman makes his Captain America rise straight up. The sight of his bald eagle makes her want to stand and recite the Pledge of Allegiance.

RATING:

CAPTAIN MARVEL

ORIGIN: Captain Marvel is a classic character from the golden age of comic books. Captain Marvel's secret identity is that of a teenager, who gets his wish by being able to transform into the super-powered hero whenever he wants.

REASON: Likewise, your Captain Marvel's teenage days may be back in the past, but when it comes to sex he has the appetite of a horny teenager.

RATING:

COLOSSUS

ORIGIN: Colossus is the strongest member of the X-Men. This immense Russian mutant can turn his body into invulnerable steel, but despite his power he is an artist and pacifist who uses his strength only for defense. If he sounds too good to be true, that's because he is. He's a comic-book character after all.

REASON: This colossal cock is huge, but there is more to a man with a Colossus than just a hard cock. He's a Renaissance man with a passion for the best things in life—especially women—so close those iron curtains, do a shot of vodka, and melt the cold war with some hot sex.

RATING:

DICK TRACY

ORIGIN: Dick Tracy is the cartoon cop with a square jaw and rock-hard fist. He doesn't have any special powers, but he's tough, smart, and knows how to treat a dame right.

REASON: A Dick Tracy is a private "dick" who will begin investigating the mystery of the disappearing clothes as soon as he tracks you down. You might as well turn yourself in and enjoy the cavity search.

RATING:

ELONGATED MAN

ORIGIN: Elongated Man is a DC Comics classic hero who can stretch and twist his body to incredible lengths and remarkable shapes. Does he sound familiar? That's because he's not the only hero with super-stretch powers. There's Mr. Fantastic, Plastic Man, Elastigirl—enough to create the world's most flexible superhero team.

REASON: An Elongated Man can stretch to incredible lengths and is able to twist into remarkable positions that give a woman extra-long orgasms. Ladies, this dick will touch you in a way no penis ever has before!

RATING:

THE FLASH

ORIGIN: The Flash is a classic comic-book character with the ability to move at nearly the speed of light.

REASON: Sure, super-speed is a useful ability for a superhero—chase a runaway train, run so fast he can turn back time—but it's horrible for a penis. Sometimes women wish their guys would just hurry up and get it over with, but not all the time. Sometimes a woman needs a dude who can control himself and take care of her first without prematurely e-*flash*-ulating.

RATING:

GHOST RIDER

ORIGIN: The comic-book character Ghost Rider is an undead motorcycle-riding spirit with a flaming skull for a head. By day he's stuntman Johnny Blaze, but after making a deal with the devil he can call upon the power of a demon to fight crime. He's a real hell's angel.

REASON: The real-life Ghost Rider isn't nearly so scary sounding as his comic-book origin, and he leaves much less of an impression. His pumps are so soft a girl won't even know when he's there, even when he's inside of her. This cock desperately needs more throttle in his engine, so for your own sake let him find somebody else to be his biker girl.

RATING: 🌀

THE GREAT CORNHOLIO

ORIGIN: In the MTV cartoon *Beavis and Butthead*, when Beavis gets too much caffeine and sugar, his arms go up, he pulls his shirt over his head, and he starts spouting gibberish that vaguely sounds like Span-

ish. He has become his alter ego "the Great Cornholio."

RATING: We love Beavis, but he is not just a dim bulb; he's a broken bulb. A penis named Cornholio has an obsession with "bungholes," which explains why he goes straight for a girl's rear end. Ladies, we suggest you keep feeding this dick sugar and give him the okay to play with your butt-head.

RATING:

HELLBOY

ORIGIN: Big, red, and demonic, Hellboy was born in the underworld but transported to Earth and raised by a scientist. Now he keeps mankind safe from evil while wise-cracking his way through his adventures against the paranormal.

REASON: A man with a Hellboy is a tough guy with a kid's spirit. He's faithful to his girlfriend, even though he bumbles his way through their relationship. These guys are lovable lugs that screw up a lot on their way to your heart. A Hellboy may look scary, but its fire-y heat will make a lucky lady melt in the bedroom.

RATING:

HULK

ORIGIN: In the comics, when David Banner gets angry he turns into the Incredible Hulk, a big, green, unthinking beast.

REASON: In real life a guy with a Hulk is a mild-mannered dude who becomes so overwhelmed by passion that he turns into a sexual animal. There are some occasions—okay a lot of occasions—when being ravished is just what a girl wants, but if she's looking for a romantic night of soft lovemaking, the Hulk won't

do. Once the guy rips off his pants, the Hulk just starts pounding.

RATING:

THE HUMAN TORCH

ORIGIN: The Human Torch is an original member of the first family of superheroes, the Fantastic Four. Astronaut Johnny Storm gained the ability to turn his body to flame (accompanied by his catchphrase, "Flame on!") and control fire after being barraged by cosmic rays. The Torch's powers are an extension of his brash, hotheaded temperament, so when it comes to his relationships, he naturally tends to burn bridges.

REASON: The Human Torch is a great name for a penis who comes with a blast of red-hot fun. The fiery emotional state of the man attached to him may cause a lot of drama in your relationship, but this dick's passion for you is flaming. You're guaranteed to hold on to this cock like the eternal flame of the sex Olympics.

RATING:

ICEMAN

ORIGIN: Iceman is a mutant with the power to convert his body into solid ice armor and freeze objects and even the air itself into ice. He is one of the original X-Men, created in 1963 by comic-book impresario Stan Lee, and has remained one of the series' most popular characters continuing through the *X-Men* film franchise.

REASON: A man with an Iceman starts a relationship as a warm and fuzzy lover who showers his partner with hugs and kisses. However, he has a limit to how much intimacy he can handle and the sex eventually turns chilly and cold.

RATING:

IRON MAN

ORIGIN: Marvel Comics' super-rich playboy character Tony Stark created the Iron Man suit to fight super-villains and impress women.

REASON: The comic Iron Man needs a suit of super-armor to be a hero, but in bed a penis called Iron Man is as heavy as iron, and as hot as molten metal. The only suit he needs to wear is made of latex. Ladies, let a guy with this dick do a sexual triathlon all over your body.

RATING:

MR. INCREDIBLE

ORIGIN: The Incredible family in the titular Pixar movie is a team of superheroes. What makes them special is that they're a nuclear family with nuclear-strength powers. Mr. Incredible has a super-strong body, but his strongest muscle is his big heart that has endless depth for his family members.

REASON: Mr. Incredible belongs to a perfect guy. He's strong, courageous, and will do whatever is necessary to "take care" of the one he loves.

RATING:

MR. FANTASTIC

ORIGIN: Mr. Fantastic is the leader of Marvel Comics' superhero team the Fantastic Four. He's also a husband and father. His super-ability allows him to stretch any part of his body to any length or size.

REASON: A guy with a Mr. Fantastic is one who will bend over backwards for his lady and his family. Plus, this super-dick can stretch out to superhuman size. Fantastic indeed!

RATING:

NIGHTCRAWLER

ORIGIN: Nightcrawler has been a popular member of the X-Men team since he first appeared in the comic books in 1975. This superhero is a mutant covered in blue fur who can teleport anywhere in the world. Despite his odd looks, he's a refined gentleman.

REASON: A real-life Nightcrawler is a penis that wants sex in the middle of the night, waking his lover up from her slumber for a midnight rendezvous. He teleports into her bed for a quickie and then disappears into the night.

RATING:

THE PUNISHER

ORIGIN: The Punisher is the anti-superhero of the Marvel Comics universe. When his innocent family was killed by the mob, Frank Castle died, and the Punisher was born. Created during a time when urban violence was making New York City seem like a war zone, the Punisher represents the revenge fantasies of every crime victim. This vigilante doesn't have any special powers and he doesn't wear a cape, but he does carry enough weaponry to equip a small army. When the system fails he uses these weapons to mete out his own version of justice. He's a one-man, ultraviolent A-Team.

REASON: The Punisher belongs to the guy who comes to a date armed with nipple clips and a whip. If a girl's idea of "staying in tonight" means being tied up in an S & M dungeon, then the Punisher could be the penis for her.

RATING:

SPAWN

ORIGIN: Spawn is the antihero of a dark comic-book series. He was a man who was killed and then resurrected as a hero with demonic powers. He now lives on earth and struggles to balance his good and evil sides.

REASON: If a penis has a struggle between good and evil then it may be a Spawn. This dick loves romantic, sweet sex, but he also likes to get naughty. A slow and sexy make-out session is right up his alley . . . as long as it's followed up with a little oral and anal sex mixed in with some S & M. As long as the sex is good keep this one around, but if his demon side gets too unbalanced, you may need an exorcism to get rid of him.

RATING:

SPEED RACER

ORIGIN: Speed Racer has been speeding around racetracks and winning races with his super-fast,

Mach 5 car since the 1960s. He's cornered the market on psychedelic, Japanese racecar drivers.

REASON: Speed might be fantastic at winning races, but it's not so good when it comes to lovin'. A speedy guy with a Speed Racer may want to hurry up sex and cross the finish line as soon as possible, but that won't win any woman's heart. Park this cock in the pit stop permanently.

RATING: 🍆

SPIDEY

ORIGIN: Wimpy Peter Parker gained the suped-up powers of a spider when a radioactive spider bit him. Luckily he absorbed all the cool powers and nothing too weird, because he'd be a pretty scary hunk if he had eight arms.

REASON: Spiderman is the friendly neighborhood super-cock, a real swinger in the sack. Spidey will have you climbing up the walls so long as you let him keep his mask on in bed. With a flick of his wrist he will shoot his sticky web all over you and bring you home in his strong arms.

RATING: 🍆

SUPERMAN

ORIGIN: DC Comics' most famous superhero was sent to Earth from the dying planet of Krypton as a baby. He is super-fast, super-strong, and super-perfect.

REASON: Superman is faster than a speeding bullet, more powerful than a jackhammer, and able to leap into your bed in a single bound. You may think that this dick is as mild-mannered as Clark Kent, but when he gets behind closed bedroom doors he hardens up into a Man of Steel. A penis named Superman is so unbelievable in bed that he must be from another world. His only kryptonite is you!

RATING:

THE THING

ORIGIN: The heroic Thing is a member of the Fantastic Four. His human body was transformed into dense orange stone in an epic sci-fi accident. His girlfriend was smart enough to stay with him once she found out every part of his body had grown to sci-fi proportions.

REASON: The Thing is a great name for a stalactite-like outcropping in a dude's superhero Underoos. This guy's whole body is like rock-hard stone, so his woman can climb all over him. She doesn't need to worry about falling to the ground when she's got a strong grip on this Thing.

RATING:

THE TICK

ORIGIN: The silly superhero the Tick is a goofy satire of people who put on costumes to fight crime. The Tick series was ahead of its time. It was making fun of superheroes years before comic-book movies became box-office juggernauts.

REASON: A real-life tick digs his way under the skin and causes itching and scratching. A Tick in the bedroom does the same. He tries to burrow into a woman's body, while his owner tries to burrow into her life. This dick is only good for a rash and trip to the doctor. Spray it with bug spray to get rid of it.

RATING:

TWO-FACE

ORIGIN: Two-Face is a perennial thorn in Batman's side. A tragic figure inspired by Dr. Jekyll and Mr. Hyde, Two-Face was originally the morally upstanding district attorney of Gotham City, Harvey Dent. Dent goes insane after acid destroys half his face, and thereafter makes his decisions based on a flip of a coin.

REASON: Everyone has met an unpredictable penis that is hot and horny one night and is limp and lazy the next. It's impossible to last with this dick because you never know what side of this schizophrenic schlong you're going to get. If he doesn't get stable quick, put the straightjacket on your relationship with this penis.

RATING:

WOLVERINE

ORIGIN: Wolverine is a superstar in the comic-book world. He has sharp claws and an unbreakable skeleton given to him as part of an evil government experiment. Who knew that a short, hairy Canadian would become so popular? He is arguably the most famous of the X-Men, and why not, with that big cigar of his?

REASON: A guy with a Wolverine is short but thick, hairy in a manly way, and stubborn with a dash of endless endurance. Those aren't bad characteristics for a guy that can't wait to get his claws into his ladylove. This dude is tough, but has a romantic side he rarely displays for certain special women. He can repair any wound with his uncanny super-healing ability, but not a broken heart, so treat him with care. In addition, this dude's Wolverine gets so hard when he's with a woman he loves that she'll swear it was hardened in a fortunate government experiment.

RATING:

ZORRO

ORIGIN: Zorro is a swordsman, who is like the Robin Hood of eighteenth-century Spanish California. He dresses like a bandit but he uses his skills to defend the powerless against evil villains. He first appeared in a pulp magazine in 1919 and has appeared in dozens of books, shows, and films.

REASON: Zorro's sword skills are unmatched, and his name means "fox" in Spanish. So a foxy guy (preferably in a mask) who leaves a *Z* mark on a woman's body has a penis that deserves to be called Zorro. Enjoy the sword fight. Viva Zorro!

RATING:

Appendicks
PENIS JOKES

Naming a penis should be a fun experience in itself, but you may need some help breaking the ice and setting the mood for a good time. In this appendicks we've included some classic penis jokes to get in the spirit to name a penis. You may remember hearing a few of them from the school playground, so some are admittedly groaners, but hopefully these oldies, but goodies will get a chuckle out of you too. After all, it's all in good fun!

A teacher walks into her classroom to find the word *penis* chalked in small letters on the board. She's a bit embarrassed, so she doesn't say anything, but rubs it out and goes on with the class.

The next day when she comes in, she finds the same thing again—penis, this time written slightly larger. So she rubs it out again, and goes on with the lesson.

Again, the next day, in even larger letters, there is the word penis on the chalkboard. With a red face, she rubs it out and goes on with the lesson.

Well, this goes on for a whole week, and every day the word *penis* gets bigger.

Finally, on Friday she goes into the classroom, and this time, the chalkboard reads: "See, the harder you rub it, the bigger it gets!"

***

A lonely woman, aged seventy, decides that it was time to get married. She puts an ad in the local paper that reads:

Husband Wanted!
Must be in my age group (seventies),
Must not beat me,
Must not run around on me,
And must still be good in bed!
All applicants please apply in person.

The next day she hears the doorbell. Much to her dismay, she opens the door to see a gray-haired gentleman with no arms or legs sitting in a wheelchair. The old woman says, "You're not really asking me to consider you, are you? Just look at you. . . . You have no legs!" The old man smiles and says, "Therefore I cannot run around on you!"

She snorts. "You don't have any hands either!" Again the old man smiles, "Nor can I beat you!"

She raises an eyebrow and gazes at him intently. "Are you still good in bed?" With that, the old gentleman leans back, beams a big broad smile, and says, "I rang the doorbell, didn't I?"

Mom took Little Johnny to the doctor for lacerations on his penis.

Doctor: How did such a thing happen?

Johnny: It's that damn neighbor girl, Susie. Her braces are too darned sharp.

***

A little boy and a little girl are in the woods. The little girl asks the boy, "What is a penis?" The boy replies, "I don't know." Then he hears his mom calling him for lunch. He goes home and eats his lunch. He sees his dad on the couch and goes up to him and asks, "What is a penis?" His dad whips his out and says to the boy, "This is a penis, and as a matter of fact, this is the perfect penis."

The boy leaves to go find his friend and brings her to the woods. The girl again asks him what a penis is. He whips out his penis and says to her, "This is a penis, and if it was two inches smaller, it would be the perfect penis!"

***

A young boy and his grandfather go fishing one afternoon. After a couple of hours, the grandfather opens a can of beer. The grandson says, "Grandpa, can I have a sip of your beer?" His grandfather looks at him and says, "Grandson, is your penis long enough to touch your ass?" The grandson replies, "No!"

"Then you're not old enough," says the grandfather.

A couple of more hours go by, and the grandfather lights a cigarette. Again the grandson notices and asks, "Grandpa, can I have a cigarette?" The grandfather replies, "Is your penis long enough to touch your asshole?" Again the grandson replies, "No!"

"Well you're not big enough to smoke yet," says the grandfather.

It starts to get late, so the grandfather decides to pack it up and head for home. On their way, they stop at a store and the grandfather buys two lottery tickets. He gives one to his grandson. Grandpa scratches his off, but didn't win anything. The grandson scratches his off and wins $10,000. Grandpa is happy and surprised that his grandson won, and he asks, "Are you going to give some of that money to grandpa?" The boy looks at him and replies, "Grandpa, is your penis big enough to touch your ass?" Grandpa looks at him for a moment, then answers, "Yes!"

"Good, then go fuck yourself!"

***

A coroner was working late one night. It was his job to examine the dead bodies before they were sent off to be buried or cremated. As he examined the body of Bernie Schwartz, who was about to be cremated, he made an amazing discovery: Bernie Schwartz had the longest penis he had ever seen!

"I'm sorry, Mr. Schwartz," said the mortician, "but I can't send you off to be cremated with a tremendously huge penis like this. It has to be saved for posterity."

And with that the coroner used his tools to remove the dead man's schlong. The coroner stuffed his prize into a briefcase and took it home. The first person he showed was his wife.

"I have something to show you that you won't believe," he said, and opened his briefcase.

"Oh my god!" she screamed, "Bernie Schwartz is dead!"

***

What's the difference between your paycheck and your dick?

You don't have to beg your wife to blow your paycheck!

***

A guy walks into a bar.

Guy: Hey, barkeeper, give me a beer.

Barkeeper: Tell you what, if you can make that horse out there laugh, I will give you a free beer and $500.

So the guy walks outside and whispers to the horse. The horse laughs. The guy walks back in.

Guy: Where's my $500 and free beer?

Barkeeper: Alright, double or nothing says you can't make that horse cry.

The guy walks outside again. The barkeep chuckles to himself as he's cleaning a glass and misses what the guy does, but he hears the horse crying. The guy comes back in.

Guy: Alright, where's my $1000 and two free beers?

Barkeeper: What did you say to make the horse laugh?

Guy: I told him I have a bigger penis than him.

Barkeeper: What did you do to make him cry?

Guy: I showed him.

***

There were three babies in a woman's womb, and they were discussing what they would like to be when they were out in the world and grown up.

The first one said, "I wanna be a plumber." The others laughed at this and asked why he wanted be a plumber. He replied, "So I can fix the pipes in here, they're kinda leaky."

The second one said, "I wanna be an electrician." The others thought this was kind of silly too and asked why. The second baby answered, "So I can get some lights in here; it's dark!"

The third one said, "I wanna be a boxer." The others thought this was hilarious and laughed for a full five minutes before asking, "Why in God's name do you want to be a boxer?"

"So," he said proudly, "I can beat the hell out of that bald guy who keeps coming in here and spitting on us."

***

One day, an old man and woman are talking in a rest home. Out of nowhere the woman says, "I can guess your age."

The man doesn't believe her, but tells her to go ahead and try.

"Pull down your pants," she says.

He doesn't understand why, but he does it anyway. She inspects his dick for a few minutes and then says, "You're eighty-four years old."

"That's amazing," the man says. "How did you know?"

"You told me yesterday."

***

Two deaf people get married. During the first week of marriage, they find that they are unable to communicate in the bedroom when they turn off the lights because they can't see each other using sign language. After several nights of fumbling around and misunderstandings, the wife decides to find a solution.

"Honey," she signs, "Why don't we agree on some simple signals? For instance, at night, if you want to have sex with me, reach over and squeeze my left breast one time. If you don't want to have sex, reach over and squeeze my right breast one time."

The husband thinks this is a great idea and signs back to his wife, "Great idea. Now, if you want to have sex with me, reach over and pull on my penis one time. If you don't want to have sex, reach over and pull on my penis fifty times."

***

A man goes into a drug store and asks the cashier for some condoms. The cashier asks, "What size?"

The man replies, "Size? I didn't know they came in sizes."

"Yes, they do," she says. "What size do you want?"

"Well, gee, I don't know," the man answers.

The lady is used to this, so she tells him to go to the backyard and measure his penis by sticking it into each of the three holes in the fence. While the man is back there, the lady sneaks around to the other side of the fence and spreads her legs behind each hole as the man tests it. When they return, the cashier asks, "What will it be? Small, medium, or large?"

The man replies, "To hell with the condoms. Give me a hundred feet of that fence back there!"

***

What did the elephant say to the naked man?

How do you breathe through that thing?

***

Q. What's the speed limit of sex?
A. Sixty-eight, because at sixty-nine you have to turn around.

***

Bob and his wife just finished having sex one night.

After catching their breath during that postcoital state, Bob said to his wife, "Tell me something that will make me happy and sad at the same time."

His wife paused and then said, "Okay, you have the biggest penis of all your friends."

***

What did one testicle say to the other?
Hey! Who's the dick in the middle?

***

If I had a rooster and you had a donkey and your donkey ate my rooster, what would you have?

My cock in your ass.

***

How do you make your wife scream after an orgasm?

Wipe your dick on the curtains.

ABOUT THE AUTHORS

Saryn Chorney is the Managing Editor of MSN's Wonderwall.com. Her online career began as Editor-in-Chief at Alloy.com. She was the founding Features Editor at Usmagazine.com, as well as the Weddings and Dating columnist for the *New York Post*, where she also contributed entertainment stories. Saryn has written for *People*, *Paper Magazine*, iVillage.com, Ellegirl.com, *YourTango*, and *Madatoms*. She has a BA in Communications and Film Studies from UPENIS—just kidding, UPENN.

Before writing this book, **David Rosenthal** represented actors, writers, and directors while working at a Beverly Hills–based talent management firm. He also helped produce the Starz comedy series *Hollywood Residential*. David has a BA in Psychology from Penn State University and a MS in Psychology from Rensselaer Polytechnic Institute. He's had a penis his entire life.

Want Some More?

Hit up our humor blog, The Daily Bender, to get your fill of all things funny—be it subversive, odd, offbeat, or just plain mean. The Bender editors are there to get you through the day and on your way to happy hour. Whether we're linking to the latest video that made us laugh or calling out (or bullshit on) whatever's happening, we've got what you need for a good laugh.

If you like our book, you'll love our blog. (And if you hated it, "man up" and tell us why.) Visit The Daily Bender for a shot of humor that'll serve you until the bartender can.

Sign up for our newsletter at

www.adamsmedia.com/blog/humor

and download our Top Ten Maxims No Man Should Live Without.